Words Are All You've Got!

The Professional's Guide To Effective Writing!

All Of The Writing Advice And Grammar You
<u>Need</u> In Order To Be Professional, And
Nothing More!

Andy X. Ash is the author of the novel, *Anthems Of The Blood And The Marrow*, and the short story collection, *Villains Among Us,* written under the pseudonym, Tombstone Kane. You can find his work at, www.tombstonekane.com.

A passionate and life long student of the English language, psychology, and marketing, he here takes on his other great love, teaching, to the masses in order to help everyone improve their communication skills and perhaps even inspire some to begin their own life long obsessions with the power and possibilities of language, and, specifically, the written word.

You can find more about Andy and the *Great Human Skills* collection at, www.greathumanskills.com.

<u>Table Of Contents</u>

Section 4: An Overview Of The Parts Of Speech

Section 5: Expansions On The Parts Of Speech

<u>Section 6: Common Errors Made When Writing</u>

Section 1:

All The Advice You Need

Let's begin by taking a look at who this book is written for, why language is so important, what kind of communication habits may be standing in the way of your success, and how you can start harnessing words to your advantage in every aspect of your life.

Introduction

The Professional's Guide To Effective Writing!

This is not another boring grammar book . . . mostly. This book is intended as a guide for you, the professional realtor, the sales person, the software developer, the marketer, the blogger, (the professional of any profession), which contains all of the writing advice and grammar you NEED in order to be professional, and nothing more!

And why should there be? Are you aiming to teach English grammar in a foreign country? Well, good, because this book probably has everything you need to get started with that too, so go on and diversify your skills you wonderful humanitarian!

You see, some people will try to convince you that you need a professor's level of grammatical knowledge in order to be any good at writing, but any good writer will tell you that it's important not to confuse grammar with writing, and that although one does need a sound understanding of basic grammar in order to write, the art of writing itself stands firm as an individual pursuit that benefits far more from life experiences and rich imaginations than it does from knowing more grammatical rules. (That said, some of us are still suckers for the too often dreaded grammatical tomes).

The reality is that few people actually benefit from an intensive deep dive into the complexities of the English language in their day to day lives. Do you, the professional, need to know what an *Asyndetonic Compound Sentence* is in order to send your client an email, or write up a contract, or come up with a great headline? I'm willing to bet not. There are, however, some general guidelines, tips, tricks, and rules that you probably should know in order to keep you from coming across as an amateur, because let's be honest, no one likes that, and those who like it least are the people you're trying to convince that it's a good idea for them to fork over their hard earned cash for your hard learned skills and services.

The point here is that a little bit of knowledge can make a tremendous contribution to your success in any field you chose to pursue. In fact, saying, (or writing), the correct thing in the correct way, (as we'll soon explore), will often be the difference between someone signing your contract, clicking on your ad, using your software, responding to your email, handing you their money . . . or not.

It's a cruel world out there and if you're eyeing success in any sort of professional endeavor in order to provide for yourself and your family, then your first step should be right here, learning the basics of communication through the uniquely human and enormously powerful art of writing. You'll be using it every day, after all, so you may as well learn to use it with a level of confidence that will shine through to everyone you come into contact with.

So, welcome. I hope this little book enriches your life and career with the profound value I have striven to imbue every page with, and that you will use it to help yourself achieve every goal you aim for now and in the future.

To your success . . . let's begin!

<u>The Wonderful World Of Words</u>

Let us first take a moment to consider the true power that is contained in the words we use every day.

The truth is that words can change the reality of your life. Naturally, many people express a fair bit of skepticism over a statement like that, because, as they say, *they're just words*.

Just words! Do you believe that? Are words simply abstract concepts we sound out to each other through various hisses and clicks and clucks in order to establish a primitive form of communication, or are they the true implements that daily determine those who end up the victors and those the victims?

Let's consider the role words have played in your own life for a moment. Think back, have you ever said something you couldn't take back? Do you remember what reality was like before that moment, and what it was like after it? Have you ever told someone that you loved them, or that you hated them, or that you were worried about them? Have you ever begged for forgiveness, pleaded for a chance, prayed for a break? Have you ever read a book that changed your life? Have you ever been called an offensive name, or been mocked and/or ridiculed? How did that make you feel? Did the words used not affect your reality? Did they not change the way you perceived certain people, the place in which you lived, the things around you?

The truth about reality is that it isn't so much about what's out there that matters; it's about how we FEEL about what's out there that makes all the difference, and what we FEEL are WORDS.

Imagine, then, the profound effect you could have on your own life if you woke up every morning and began telling yourself that you felt great instead of tired. That you are capable, strong, and confident, instead of unqualified, weak, and depressed. What if you began telling your significant other that he or she is beautiful, special, and important instead of saying nothing at all? What if you offered a word of encouragement to a colleague, a congratulatory note to an acquaintance, a friendly greeting to a stranger? What if you suddenly spoke, (and wrote), with enthusiasm, with positivity, and with energy? How do you think the people around you would react? How would your clients? Even more importantly . . . how would your potential clients? What about your employer, or your employees? Your co-workers? Your friends?

Are you beginning to see the enormous impact just a few words can have on your life? *They're just words,* is an unacceptable description of the tools we use every day in order to communicate our thoughts, hopes, dreams, goals, and feelings, and the mere knowledge of the power is enough to start one on the path of understanding just how easily success or failure can be achieved with little more than proper communication skills. Words are important, and more than that, they are profoundly powerful. They indeed do have the power of reality, and using a new, more correct, more descriptive, and/or more powerful word will change not only how you think and feel about the world, but also how those who come into contact with you think and feel about it. A single word, the correct word, or combination of words, <u>can change your life</u>.

Additionally, being aware of the words you use when writing and while in conversation ensures that you're always with a degree of control, because you can reveal and conceal as much or as little as you deem necessary in order to steer the communication toward the outcome YOU DESIRE.

The Miracle Of Writing

Let's now take a look at an astonishing feat that can only be accomplished with a combination of words and the human mind. We call this miracle, writing.

You see, the mere fact that we are capable of reading and writing an assortment of symbolic strokes on a page in order to convey thoughts, feelings, ideas, and meanings with the same nonchalance as taking a breath is something so profoundly confounding that it escapes all attempts at a satisfactory philosophical explanation.

Take a moment to think about the true meaning of this rather mundane ability. Think about the fact that we can not only communicate a vast array of human experiences to each other, but we can pass on our knowledge, ideals, and experiences for literally thousands of years into the future, in hundreds of languages, so that they can be built upon and expanded on by people we will never meet, and in order to solve problems we will never be able to even conceive of.

It's romantic, sure, but do you really think a device like the computer could ever have been achieved without our ability to pass down written knowledge and then build upon it? Do you think we could have cities, cars, airplanes, spaceships, satellites, or any other of the truly amazing things we humans have been able to conjure up from nature without writing?

There was a time when memory was considered an art form in its own right, and the introduction of books, (writing), was declared a heresy to this noble art. The mind was meant to be the pristine receptacle that contained all of the world's knowledge and truths, and no defamation or challenge of its virtuous standing should exist. Imagine then, what our world would look like today if such an idea, (of which we are, ironically, only aware of because of writing), had been enforced.

Luckily, that was not the case, and the reality is that the world of today has been shaped by writing. It has created it, altered it, and challenged it with arguments of religion, politics, entertainment, philosophy, mathematics, music, law, art, society, and more. Our words, you see, have the ability to make reality malleable, for they allow us hopes and dreams, and they cause us fear and dread, and they can uplift us or tear us down, support or chastise us, bless or condemn us. Most importantly, however, they give us the ability to escape into worlds filled with nothing but possibilities, fantasies, extravagancies, fictions and truths.

Sure, the scribbles change from country to country, and sometimes even from street to street, and some languages, like Latin, conquer the world and then disappear forever, but what never changes is the possibilities, the freedoms, and the sheer powers writing bestows upon the human race.

Language is a dynamic thing, evolving simultaneously with us, but what is it, really?

Well . . . it's a genuine form of magic! Imagine yourself hosted on a remote island by a tribe of natives who've never had contact with the modern world. They can communicate, of course, with their voices and movements, but they've not yet conceived of the written word. You decide to try a little experiment to see how receptive they might be to such an amazing idea, so you beckon the chief to your side and tell him:

"Honorable friend. What if I told you that I could make my friend Lester over there jump up and down on one leg without speaking a single word to him or making any commanding movements?"

The chief considers your proposal a moment and shakes his head. "Impossible," he decides.

"Fair enough," you say. "But just to keep things honest and prove that none of it was arranged beforehand as a trick, tell me, what would you like my friend Lester to do if not jump up and down on one foot?"

Pursing his lips, a deep, brooding frown contorts his face for a moment, and then his brow arches high, brightening his face, and he says: "I want the strange man to dance."

"Very well," you say. "Observe."

On a piece of paper you write: Dear Lester, our kind host, the chief, would like you to do him the honor of performing a dance.

You hand the note to the chief for inspection. He brings it up to his ear and listens for whispers. He sniffs it, licks it, rubs its texture between his fingers and decides that yes, indeed, there doesn't seem to be any sort of trickery at work.

"Please," you say. "Hand that note to Lester and watch what happens."

Lester receives the note, reads it, shrugs his shoulders, stands, and begins to dance in place. Astonished, the chief doesn't react with the profound curiosity you'd expected. Instead, he and his tribe display a tremendous fear of you both, and before you can exert any more of your incredible influence over any of his people, he has you both bound, beaten, and burned alive.

Magic, here, is responsible for your untimely deaths.

It's easy to take writing for granted in today's world, especially in developed countries where standardized education is available to every child regardless of economic or societal factors. Writing, indeed, has become one of the most basic and fundamental skills of the human race, and though it can be done well enough to get by, when it's done with care and confidence, the results can often seem as magical as it did to our terrified chief only a moment ago.

<u>Only One Word Matters: Credibility</u>

YOUR business will fail without credibility. Of course, building a reputation for being the best, fastest, cheapest, easiest service in the business involves far more than just the words you use in your professional and every day communications, because you do provide a service, after all, and the quality of that service is often enough to provoke word of mouth to be passed on to your satisfied clients' friends and family.

However, when it comes to attracting a prospective client, one searching for a business which can provide the service he/she needs without any previous information about your business, the words you use are quite often the only things that do matter. Before first contact ever occurs, those words establish your credibility in your prospect's mind, and if they fail to do so, your door will never open, your phone will never ring, and your inbox will never ding.

Don't believe me? Try this:

"Don't miss this beautiful lakefront property for an great price! Their is a new dock in the water, a nice fire pit in the backyard, and their is a store just around the corner for bate and tackle. Call me today for a viewing!"

First off, if you don't see the unforgivable grammatical errors in this short paragraph, don't worry, because that's exactly why this book was written, and that's exactly why you've made an excellent decision by reading it!

Now, back to the property ad, put yourself in the shoes of someone looking for a new family home. You're scanning through large collections of photos and prices, which is what first attracts you to this listing, and then you come across this paragraph with its misuse of the indefinite article "an", and the blatant use of the incorrect form of "their", (twice), and its mis-spelling of the word "bate", and suddenly you're faced with the question: should I call this agent and arrange a viewing?

Should you?

Let's try another one:

"I am always available to provide you with a free quote for custom jobs. You're satisfaction is our first concern and its our guarantee!"

Granted, many people may not even notice anything wrong with this and your phones may continue to ring unabated. But people like me notice, and there are lots of people like me out there, and the mere fact that "you're" is a contraction instead of the possessive you intended, and "its" is a possessive instead of the contraction you intended, (Don't worry, these are easier than you may think), is enough to give some of us pause to reflect on if the quality of your work or service is on par with your writing skills. The fact of the matter is that these errors *do* make a difference, because these are the most basic elements of English grammar.

Let's try one more example to really drive home the point:

Imagine you're on your favorite movie ratings site. Scrolling down the page you see various headlines hemmed in with varying amounts of stars, and after reading a few of the high ratings, you decide to have a gander at the criticisms. Down to a single star review you scroll and start to read something along the lines of:

"This movie was so much worst than the last one, plus it had that big italian guy with the goofy eyes. Anyway, bad, bad, bad. Don't see. Wast of time. So not intelligent but all the way stupid. I want my money back. "

The question is how much weight are you willing to give to this person's credibility given the spelling and grammatical mistakes? Are you likely to place any value whatsoever on this review? Do you even understand what this person is trying to say?

I wish I could tell you that this is just some contrived example I came up with in order to illustrate the point, but the truth is that this type of nonsensical, nearly unintelligible writing is everywhere on the internet, and this type of scoffing write-off of your credibility is exactly what happens when your own professional writings suffer from poor grammatical and stylistic grace.

We'd all like to believe that we live in a judgement-free and respectful world, but we don't, and every time you sit down to compose an ad, or post something on your business's social media page, or send a quote or an email to a customer and your writing is littered with errors, you're more apt to cause doubts about your ability to deliver the services you promise rather than establish a level of trust that will result in additional, or perhaps even current, business transactions.

It's important to realize that in today's world, nearly half, if not more, of our daily communications with other people happens through writing. We write blogs, send emails, text, fill out forms, write advertising copy, comment code, post on social media, write quotes, etc . . . If the old adage that said that 70 to 80 percent of all communication is non-verbal ever had any truth, it certainly fails to apply in the 21st century.

That being said, it's also important to realize that anyone, everyone, can learn to write. It isn't some obscure magic people are born with, it's a skill like any other, and all it requires, like any other skill, is practice and perseverance. It takes discipline and mistakes. With a little time and effort, you too will be able to confidently write effective sales quotes, emails, advertising copy, and whatever else you want to tackle.

Think of the journey you're now taking as if you are an orchard farmer. Here you are planting seeds, and every day hereafter you will tend to the ground, you will water, fertilize, and wait. You will do these things with patience and care, because unlike a crop of corn or wheat, which needs to be reseeded year after year, the mature orchard trees you cultivate will eventually provide you with fruit for the rest of your life.

The time and effort you put into this will be small change compared to the new world of possibilities your skills will provide you with.

<u>Confidence = Communication Skills</u>

Are you a confident person? Have you always been? If you aren't, why aren't you? Why do some people seem to naturally exude an aura of confidence while others seem to lack all semblance of anything that could even remotely be considered confidence?

Perhaps it's never occurred to you, but if you take a moment to think about it I think you'll find that confident people tend to have great, and sometimes extraordinary, communication skills. They can seemingly speak to anyone and convince some of their ideas, and command others to do their bidding, and attract yet others to hand over their money on mere promises of success.

How do they do it?

You might think that the answer to that question could fill an entire book, and perhaps it could, but fundamentally, these people's greatest asset is their ability to communicate with everyone they come into contact with. If you were to observe a great communicator in his or her natural environment, you'd find that their approach to the same subject changes dramatically according to the person they're speaking with or writing to. (A subject we'll touch on in just a bit). They adjust their language and behavior in order to best leverage the other person's state of mind, emotional state, educational level, interests, etc...

Now, that skill might need an entire book dedicated to it, and in the end we may even find that these master communicators are indeed benefitting from natural born powers; namely, an instinct or talent to read other people that simply can't be learned.

Nonetheless, if you do lack this type of natural ability, you can certainly still learn enough about how to properly communicate in order to give yourself an edge against your competition and attract people to you.

This book is primarily about writing, but I think you'll find that by understanding how to write you'll experience a boost of confidence which will immediately transfer into incredible improvements in the way you speak to others, and perhaps even in how you behave in general.

The goal in your business is to attract, retain, and repeat a customer base, and you need to accomplish that by establishing a sense of authority in your respective field. You want people to trust that you are the best in your industry, or at the very least, that you are the best choice for them because you know what you're doing, you're reliable, fair, and dedicated to helping them. None of these things will happen if you're unable to write clear, concise sentences that get to the heart of what your clients are looking for and spare them all of the superfluous asides that inevitably muddle the message you're attempting to convey.

There is an astonishing power held by those who are capable of conveying their passion for a subject, their depth of knowledge, and their vision for the future. It infects people, it drives them to try harder and to think outside the box for solutions no one had conceived of before. There is an energy that electrifies the words of the passionate and the confident, and learning how to infuse your own words with that same energy is a skill that will unlock a truly infinite potential from which you will always reap incredible rewards.

History is full of passionate men and women who rose above the societal, economical, educational, and political hurdles of their times to inspire millions and lead them toward their desired goals as though captivated by a spell. Indeed. The magic was in the words, in the passion with which they spoke and/or wrote, and the end result, in fields as varied as science, business, politics, religion, and war have often been nothing short of staggering.

You are no different. You can attract people to you with your words. All you need to do is leverage the powerful feelings that already lie within you. Dig them up and expose them, give them air, express them with courage and determination and you may just feel as though you've somehow molded the very fabric of reality around you.

Confidence is the energy with which others will identify, and the rest is up to you.

How To Write For Maximum Impact

What the "maximum impact" is, exactly, depends on your particular goals and circumstances, but there are a few things you can *always* do in order to keep your thoughts organized and your writing on point.

The first tip is to bullet point the ideas, thoughts, emotions, messages, and even certain words you'd like to use **before** you begin writing your letter, application, email, etc. In certain situations, when what you're writing really counts, it would be advisable to go even further and think seriously about the style, form, tenses, and voice you plan on using.

Fear not, all of these subjects are covered and clarified in this book.

What's important to remember is that the lack of a plan is always obvious because the resulting writing tends to come out convoluted and confused. It lacks direction, and the messages, ideas, and thoughts the writer is attempting to convey get lost in the jumble. With a little bit of practice you'll find that even if the ideas or words you jotted down aren't used in the final product, they still either contributed to it, or, even better, caused you to think of something you hadn't originally considered, often a far better point, conveyed more concisely, and with an impact even you couldn't quite clearly see in the beginning. It really is magic when it happens.

The second tip is to have empathy. Now, empathy is a word with a definition that often gets confused, (see **p. 194**), but one of its basic meanings is the ability to identify or experience vicariously the feelings, thoughts, and/or attitudes of another person. It's being able to "put yourself in someone else's shoes". It sounds simple, sure, and it's even one of the basic features of a healthy human mind, but it is also, perhaps due to social influences, one of the most mis-practiced abilities we have. People rarely ask themselves, "how would I feel about this in his/her shoes." Empathy is an essential ability for the successful novelist, for without it, proper characterization and development would be impossible, and for our purpose, the huge influence this simple question will exert on your writing cannot be understated.

In fact, we've already looked at it with the "bad movie review" example. If you're looking for a job, imagine yourself as the hiring person. If you're trying to get a sale, imagine yourself as the person receiving the quote. Tell yourself while re-reading your writing, *"I don't know the person who wrote this, so what will make me care or notice them from all the others?"* You'll be amazed at how often we humans tend to fall into the trap of thinking that other people are familiar with the reality we know, when there could be nothing further from the truth. Empathy for the purpose of writing does take practice, but doing it will work wonders for you, as it allows for more profound and personal connections to be established between you and other people.

The third tip is to write authoritatively. You'll come across books that encourage you to write using what's called the "active voice." We'll have a discussion on that subject later on, (**p. 61**), as well as a word on the importance of writing clearly and concisely, (**p. 43**), but this tip is a subtle variation of both of these later subjects. Our focus here is essentially to encourage you to say exactly what you want to say and avoid unnecessary extras.

As you'll see throughout this book, examples are often the greatest teachers.

What you want to say:

". . . So, I was thinking that maybe, if you have time this weekend, you'd like to hang out or something, maybe go clothes shopping at the new store on 111th? Let me know. Thanks."

Sure, it gets your point across, but it oozes with insecurity. If you want results, whether with your writing or in face to face conversations, you need to learn to be more assertive. Doing so will change your life forever. In the above example, you're simply trying to be too considerate of the other person, you're leaving them with too many outs, too many possibilities for dismissal. If you really want to "hang out" with this person, then what you should write is:

"I thought we could go clothes shopping at the new store on 111th this weekend. Let me know."

Short and to the point. This leaves you in a position of authority, a position that awaits a response that is *as clear and concise as your request*. It's a yes or no, and when it's structured in this way, replying with a no becomes far more difficult than it was in our first example. This new structure puts the other person on the spot, and if you want results in your life, sometimes the difference between putting someone on the spot and not is the difference between success or failure.

Naturally, the circumstances vary, so be aware of precisely what your goal is beforehand. Never be too forceful with anyone, and especially not with a potential employer or customer, but keep in mind that there is always a way to politely structure your writing in order to accomplish the same thing without seeming pushy, rude, or pretentious.

Always avoid being pushy, rude, or pretentious!

The fourth tip is to learn to read like a writer. Novelists are often given this advice, but it isn't as easy as it may at first sound. To read like a writer means to be able to disassociate yourself from the story being told and focus on how other writers have structured their sentences, what words they've used and why, what effects they have managed to produce with certain combinations of syllables or words, how they managed to communicate mood, build context, use ambiguity, etc. It isn't an easy task, but with practice and concentration you'll soon find yourself able to tell the difference between good and bad writing, as well as why something worked and why something else did not. Writing is all around you, all day, every day. Have a look with the eyes of a writer and see what happens.

The fifth and final tip of this section is a statement already presented at the beginning of this book, but it is so important to understand that it's worth reiterating. The statement is that writing isn't all about the grammar. Now, again, this may seem like something counterintuitive to state in a book that does indeed contain sections dedicated to grammar, but the truth is that writing is about communication. The grammar is necessary in order to structure the communication in effective ways, but writing, good writing, is the result of striking up a nice balance between grammar, creativity, originality, and style. No one is born a writer. Everyone has to first learn the alphabet, and then some grammar, and then the creativity, originality, and style come with experimentation and exploration.

Sometimes you just have to fill out a form, but wouldn't you like that form to also be correctly written, concise, and clear? At other times you want to make an impression, so wouldn't you want to stand out by making that impression through the experimentation of new things?

In time, you'll be able to adjust to whatever situation you're presented with, and in each you'll have the confidence to know that you can write as well as anyone else in the same situation.

<u>Your Vocabulary Is Your Identity</u>

How would you describe yourself? Are you a happy person? Are you a free spirited, kind, and caring person, or are you severe, despondent, and pessimistic? Do you look toward the future or fear the unknown? Responsible, dependable, honest, or charlatan, liar, cheat? How do other people describe you? Are you fun? Are you smart? Are you capable?

All of these words *describe* the qualities that pertain to your character. They are ascribed by other people and attained by reputation through your behavior, your actions, and most of all, through your WORDS.

The words you tell yourself, and those you tell others, define your reality.

These words become your identity. Naturally, there is going to be some variation between your opinion of yourself and the opinions other people have of you, but the point is that the words you use to describe yourself become your identity, and the words other people use to describe you become your identity *to them*.

Make no mistake. Words are capable of literally shaping your reality.

When writing, therefore, take care in choosing your words and tone, for they will make all the difference.

*"It's not **what** you said, it's **how** you said it that matters."*

It's fantastic advice to keep in mind for every word you write or speak, but in reality, *what* you say really does make all the difference.

There's another point to be made here, though, and it's that you should make an effort to *expand* your vocabulary. Learn more verbs, more descriptive adjectives, more nouns, more ways to describe the things you feel, see, touch, smell, and hear with greater depth and vivid meaning. Carrying around an expanded vocabulary in your head will help you in unlimited situations in life and render you capable of conversing with anyone, regardless of their social status, education level, or professional achievements. From formal to casual, having an expanded vocabulary will allow you to pick up the patterns of other people and speak to them on *their* level. There is a section on this subject later on called matching expectations (**p. 69**), but the idea here is a little more subtle, in that, for successful communication you need the ability to change the way you speak and the words you use depending on the person you're speaking and/or writing to. Learn the difference between formal and casual language, and use it when and where it's appropriate.

To take the idea of this section one step further and focus strictly on writing, there is a tremendous value in expanding your vocabulary when you are writing, because a limited vocabulary means you'll end up reusing the same nouns, adjectives, and verbs, over and over again to describe different things, and you'll rely on metaphors and analogies to describe things for you, sometimes with only limited success or truth, and the end result will be that your communication will be cluttered, boring, confusing, and/or just plain nonsensical. Having to reuse the same words, sometimes in the same sentence, is often a sign of poor writing skills. If you've used the adjective joyful and you want to convey a similar emotion, find a different and perhaps more accurate word for what you're trying to say. Naturally, sometimes, the same word is exactly what you need to use, but that isn't always the case.

Fine, you say. Okay, let's expand my vocabulary! How do I do that?

Well, you first do it by reading. That's right. The first rule of creative writing, (which this book isn't about, but the advice is great), is that if you want to be a great writer, then you better become a great reader. Secondly, when you're writing and you want to use a word, take a moment to first look it up in the dictionary and/or thesaurus and see what synonyms apply to the chosen word.

Beware of using certain synonyms, however, as is explained here (**p. 72**).

In conclusion, we should do a little exercise in order to really drive the point home about the direct link between vocabulary and identity, because it's one of the most important communication and psychological lessons you're ever likely to learn. Consider the following:

"Excuse me, could you point me to the nearest restroom, please?"

"Hi, there, do you know if there's a bathroom around here?"

"Hey, man, are there like, any washrooms around here?"

"Yo, dog, any pissers 'round?"

"Toilets. Where are they?"

All of these sentences are asking for the same thing, but they're doing so using different tones and different words. Did your brain automatically conjure up a different image of the person asking each of them? If it did, well, congratulations, you're totally normal and now fully aware of the point.

Your vocabulary is your identity.

<u>Power Persuasion</u>

An entire book can be, (and many are), written on the subject of persuasion. There is no room or reason for an in-depth analysis of the subject for our purpose, but given the fact that this text is primarily aimed at the professional who is trying to persuade total strangers to take notice of him/her and/or what he or she has to offer, let's take a brief overview of the subject of persuasion in order to better help you, the budding writer, form your goals and ideas *before* beginning to write.

So what is persuasion, exactly? Well, persuasion is a synonym of *influence*, and its purpose is typically aimed at influencing another person's behaviors, beliefs, intentions, motivations, and/or attitudes. A sales pitch is a form of persuasion. It is a structured, sometimes even scripted, attempt to get you, the potential customer, to purchase a specific product and/ or create awareness of a company and the rest of its available product line.

Political campaigns are highly structured, sometimes invasive, and aggressive forms of persuasion that rely on highlighting the perceived benefits of voting for one candidate over the utter horrors that could result from the election of his or her supposed untrustworthy opponent(s).

But persuasion isn't always a professional endeavor. Simply trying to convince a friend to go to a movie, or hang out, or go shopping, regardless of how little effort or awareness is involved, is still a form of persuasion.

Asking someone on a date, and hence the entire date itself is a form of persuasion, as both parties try, (hopefully), to convey the best of themselves to the other person.

Writing something like, "I think you'll find my skills and experience well suited to the position you've advertised," is exactly what persuasion is all about. It is the effort of convincing someone that they are or will be doing something that is in *their* best interest. That it's good to hire me, to date me, to vote for me, to buy my products, because ***I will add value to your life.***

And there's the heart of it.
We humans are always, in one form or another, searching for value, for meaning, for a purpose that makes things worth doing and life worth living. This search is at the core of all of our behaviors; right along with our universal friend, fear, and our resulting avoidance of it.

These two instincts are responsible for your life and for the world around you. It's hardly a new discovery. Humans have been aware of these two tremendously powerful forces for thousands of years, but like many psychological forces, they often hide right there in the open. They are things we say and do every day without realizing exactly what it is that we are saying and doing.

Stock market enthusiasts will tell you that the financial world, and for some, the entire world, runs on *fear and greed*. That may be true on a fundamental level of the financial market, but to extend that view to the rest of society is a narrow and potentially dangerous proposition. There is certainly far more complexity and influence about in the world, but for the purpose of trading stocks, these two simple emotions are often all that are needed to persuade millions of people to move trillions of dollars one way or another year after year.

The struggle we as emotional beings constantly face is the one that lies between the things we want to integrate into our lives and the things we want to keep out of them. Persuasion, (loosely), is the force that attempts to entice you to act one way or another based on either value or fear. It's why marketers are constantly telling you that you should buy their products in order to make your life easier, (value), to save yourself some money, (value), but hurry, because these prices are on for a limited time only, (fear).

Broadly speaking, persuasion has two categories which are regularly used separately as well as in combination. The first of these is called, ***Systematic Persuasion***, and it's generally defined as a process through which a person's beliefs and/or attitudes toward something or someone is challenged by *appeals to logical and reasonable arguments and conclusions*.

An example of systematic persuasion is:

"Think about it, purchasing this vehicle will save you almost $300 per month, it's a no-brainer."

Here, an appeal is made to both reason and logic, and calls for you to consider the monthly savings that will result from your decision to purchase this particular vehicle over all the others in the lot. "It's a no-brainer," makes it a purely logical decision based on the fact that this imaginary salesperson is assuming that any *reasonable* person would be more than happy to save $300 per month versus driving away in a more expensive vehicle.

The second of these is called, ***Heuristic Persuasion***, which is generally defined as a process through which a person's beliefs and/or attitudes toward something or someone is challenged by *appeals to habits and/or emotions*.

An example of heuristic persuasion is:

"Heads will turn when you drive this baby down the street."

In this case, the appeal is purely emotional. Imagine yourself driving this car! Imagine how everyone will turn to stare at you as you pass them by! They'll think you're an actor, or a professional athlete, or at the very least, rich.

So there you have it, the two very high-level, very basic facets of the psychology behind persuasion. It is a vast and fascinating subject that anyone with even the smallest interest in is strongly encouraged to learn more about. You're guaranteed to learn more about yourself, about the people around you, and about the world you live in.

How fitting, then, to end with a bit of persuasion.

But wait, you may still have an additional question at this point. Which is the most effective of the two? Is it Systematic or Heuristic persuasion that takes the cake?

Well, the answer is complicated, unclear, and difficult to determine. What is clear, however, is that both do work, separately and in combination, and probably the simplest answer to this question is to state the obvious:

It depends on the person.
Or rather, it depends on how that person *feels* at the specific point in time at which you contact them.

So go on, give it a try when you want something. Even the smallest, insignificant thing is no reason to not practice and hone your skills. Every opportunity *is an opportunity*. Make use of them.

<u>Section 2:</u>

Suggestions About Style

This section focuses on general suggestions about writing. Take note that these are not hard rules etched in stone; rather, they're general rules of thumb to help you style your writing, but their adoption will make all the difference in how you express yourself.

The next time you're writing something, anything, keep these ideas in mind.

<u>Accuracy Over Clarity</u>

It's important to clearly convey what you want in all forms of communication, but clarity takes a certain amount of accuracy in order for it to be valid. Improperly pronouncing a word, misspelling, incorrect grammar, or worst of all, simply using an inappropriate word, can make the difference between being understood and taken seriously and being misunderstood and brushed aside with some other choice opinions.

Think about it. If you mean to say white, but instead say black, whose fault is it for the misunderstanding? Is the receiving end's opinions of you erroneous? If you want a coffee, but order a slice of carrot cake, should you yell at the barista? If you'd like to ask someone out to dinner, but instead ask them to buy you dinner, or tie your shoes, or bark like a dog, should you be surprised at their lack of interest, or perhaps even anger?

Can you *sing* my book?
Did she *loose* weight?
I *past* the test.
The point here should be clear. Using the proper word, in its proper form, and placed in its proper position according to the proper grammatical rule for the specific situation can literally make reality follow either the left path, or the right. It's up to you.

So what are you saying?

<u>Be Explicit Rather Than Implicit</u>

What's meant by being explicit here isn't an encouragement to be rude in your writing; rather, it is to avoid leaving ambiguity in your writing to muddy your meaning.

Here's an example that demonstrates what ambiguity is, how it may arise, and the unintended consequences it may produce:

In your inbox is an invitation to a wedding from your friend Lina, an old friend from college you haven't seen in a few years. Surprised, you read the letter:

"You are cordially invited to join Hector Hammond and Lina Moore on their special day of matrimony on July 25th. Please RSVP below:

-Will Be Attending:
-Number of Guests:
-Attending the Ceremony and Dinner, or the Reception only:
-Comments:

Thank you and we look forward to seeing you on our special day!"

Now, a flurry of emotions pass through you about the whole thing, and as they do, you RSVP like this:

-Will Be Attending: *Yes*
-Number of Guests: *One. But maybe two.*
-Attending the Ceremony and Dinner, or the Reception only: *Ceremony & Dinner*
-Comments: *Oh my god, Lina! I'm so happy for you! I can't wait to see you. I'll try my best to make it and hopefully my S.O. can make it, and maybe my sister, you remember her from school? Anyway, I'll see if I can get some time off of work and make it down there for your big day! Hope to see you soon!*

Now, what's poor Lina to think? How clear is this response? Should she add an extra plate to the catering service? Two extra plates? Three? Are you even attending? Sure, it says yes . . . at first, but then it goes on to confuse the whole thing with if's and maybe's and hopefully's, words that are wholeheartedly indefinite and indecisive when all Lina really wanted was a definitive yes or no so she could move on and worry about other things in relation to her wedding, not about whether or not you're going to cost her, potentially, up to three extra plates and not show up.

In all your communications, and especially in professional communications, it's always kinder and far more efficient to be explicit with your intentions. Yes. No. Avoid indefinite words and then assume that the other person knows what you mean. "Oh, he knows me, he knows what I mean." No, "he" does not, and no one appreciates having to waste time and energy figuring out what exactly it is that you mean by what you said.

Think of the consequences such a small matter can have on your life. What if you're looking for a job? What if you're trying to land a big client? What if you want to date that person you've had your attentions on for the last few weeks? How clear do you want to be with your intentions?

Then be clear.

Avoid Repetition

Too often the same thing is stated again and again in the same paragraph. This common error seems to occur due to a writer's desire to emphasize a specific point, or highlight an important idea, but the result of his/her attempts ends up as many sentences that essentially repeat themselves.

Consider the following:

"I would like to express my interest in the position of <generic position> as advertised on <generic job site>.

"I think my education and experience in this field makes me an ideal match for the candidate you're seeking in order to fill this position.

"I am a reliable, punctual, and friendly person who enjoys a challenge and I think your company would be a great fit for my skills and personality.

"I'm a quick learner, and although I am not familiar with the specific accounting program you use, I am certain that I can pick it up in no time at all and become a useful addition to your team.

"I thank you in advance for your consideration and will be eagerly awaiting your reply.
Sincerely, <hopeful's name>"

Now, this person is really interested in the position, and he/she is convinced that he/she is a perfect fit for the company. So convinced, in fact, that he or she has said so at least three times: "an ideal match", "a great fit", and "a useful addition to your team". In addition, he/she has made it clear, twice within the same sentence that he or she is good at learning new skills: "I am a quick-learner", and "I can pick it up in no time at all".

Now, this may seem like a forced example just to make a point, but it isn't at all. In corporate offices around the world, letters like these make their way to hiring executives, and more often than not, they are tossed off to the side in search of candidates more capable of concise presentations. He or she really could be the very best fit for this company's position, however, he/she's inability to spot how many times he/she has repeated him or herself in order to try and emphasize that fact has, in the end, done him/her more harm than good.

So, what should a person do?
Well, the first piece of advice is to *always* re-read your letter, email, copy *before* sending it off. READ the sentences, every word of them, with concentration on the meaning of the words you've written. You'll be surprised to find how often such repetitious errors tend to crop up, especially when you're emotionally involved in the outcome of your communication.

In the case of the above mock cover letter, simply removing the repetitions would improve our hypothetical applicant's credentials immensely.

It's true what psychologists say: You only get one chance at making a first impression. This is your very first. Showing that you can properly and concisely express yourself will help you stand out and perhaps allow you to formally introduce yourself in person, putting you one step closer to achieving your goal.

"I would like to express my interest in the position of <generic position> as advertised on <generic job site>.

"I am a reliable and friendly person with the required education, experience, and skills to fulfill your needs and make a useful addition to your team.

"I thank you in advance for your consideration and will be eagerly awaiting your reply.
Sincerely, <hopeful's name>."

Figures Of Speech . . . Use At Your Own Risk

A figure of speech is defined as: "a word or phrase used in a non-literal sense for rhetorical or vivid effect" -*google dictionary.*

There are many, (many!), figures of speech, but for this book we'll focus only on the one's you're most likely to use in your every day communications.

> 1 – The Metaphor (pronounced meta - fore)
> 2 – The Simile (pronounced sea – ma - lee)
> 3 – The Hyperbole (pronounced hyper – beau - lee)
> 4 – The Oxymoron (pronounced ox – see – moron)
> 5 – The Analogy (pronounce ana - lo - gee)

You'll come across and perhaps even use these every day without realizing it, but having the ability to recognize and thus use them when appropriate can prove to be a formidable ally in your vocabulary.

The first thing you need to understand about figures of speech is that they should be used only in appropriate circumstances. In many formal settings, the use of figures of speech can be construed as immature, unqualified, or even plain offensive, depending on the recipient's expectations. If we return to our previous cover letter example (**p. 47**), we can see that in the original letter, the writer used the idiom (**p.57**), "I can *pick it up in no time at all*", which may be perfectly acceptable and reasonable to use in that situation; however, if he/she had made extensive use of figures of speech and said things like, "I'm as quick as a horse," "I think I'd fit into your company like a hand in a glove," or, "Your organization is my dream," then the effectiveness of the letter would dwindle and would seem to be wasting the hiring person's time and offending their expectations of finding a professional candidate to fill the role.

On the other hand, when writing marketing copy, or fiction, or any number of other creative type of projects, then the use of figures of speech can be extremely powerful and useful tools used to convey points, ideas, and values to other people.

Let's have a look at the most common ones.

#1: The Metaphor:

Since the purpose of this text isn't to be an exhaustive grammatical text, the simplest way to remember how a metaphor works is to generalize it and state that: a metaphor makes a DIRECT comparison WITHOUT using the words *like* or *as*.

The classic example used to explain a metaphor is a quote from William Shakespeare's play, As You Like It:

> "All the world's a stage,
> All the men and women merely players;
> They have their exits and their entrances . . ."

The metaphor in this excerpt is clear: we know the world isn't a literal stage and the men and women aren't literal players, but we can appreciate the *implied* comparison without having to make it explicit, (i.e.: the world is *like* a stage, the men and women are *like* players).

A note:

      When writing, use metaphors with care as they can easily accomplish one of two things. The first is to clarify a concept, and the second is to make it more ambiguous and therefore less clear. If it isn't evident that you're using a metaphor, or the person you're writing to can't discern its meaning, you've introduced the opportunity for miscommunication to occur between your recipient and yourself.

#2 The Simile:

      A simile is a FORM of metaphor, (there are quite a few that will not be covered in this particular book), that you are likely to come across daily. Unlike the metaphor proper, a simile makes a DIRECT comparison between two things, objects, or concepts by explicitly using words such as *like* and *as*.

Examples:
> He's as angry as a rabid dog.
> She's as curious as a cat.
> They came together like a swarm of bees.

A note:
> When using similes, make sure the comparisons you're making make sense. For example, "he's as angry as a grey rock" has no value as a description because it's comparing two disparate and completely unrelated things.

#3 The Hyperbole:

The hyperbole is a figure of speech you likely come across multiple times per day. "He dragged it for miles," is an example. "Her purse weighed a ton," is another. A hyperbole is nothing more than an exaggeration used in order to emphasize your point. It isn't meant nor intended to be taken literally. Some language enthusiasts refer to the hyperbole as *intensifiers*.

> "The guy has the strength of a gorilla."
> "I'll get it done lightning quick."

"She's an Einstein."

#4 The Oxymoron:

Oxymorons are quite common in English. They are characterized by the use of contrary statements used as modifiers. Example: "That burger was *disgustingly delicious*!", "It's a *love-hate relationship*." They are often used in order to illustrate a point or reveal a paradox in an idea, philosophy, and/or belief. This figure of speech is intended to be used on purpose by the writer or speaker, and understood as an oxymoron by the reader or listener. Note, however, that oxymorons are used all the time in English without intention. Saying things like: "crash landing," "found missing," or, "act naturally" are all oxymorons, but they also tend to convey exactly what the writer or speaker intends. The plane did, literally, "crash land."

In addition, oxymorons are particularly powerful tools when used in fiction as they provide vivid and sometimes even jarring descriptions for objects, places, people, or ideas.

"There was a *deafening silence* in the cave."
"The whole thing was a *tragic comedy*."
"That was a *near miss* incident."

#5 Analogy:

Analogy is a broad area of linguistics, (which is an area of psychology), that applies to pointing out the similarities between two things, objects, or concepts by comparison. In this sense, metaphors and similes, among others, are themselves forms of analogies. Somewhat unlike the metaphor and the simile, however, the purpose of an analogy is to explain one thing in terms of another thing by highlighting the ways in which they're alike, or the qualities they share. In essence, an analogy is more of a *logical* argument rather than a simple figure of speech. In fact, many psychologists claim that analogies are the core of human knowledge and understanding. It is the key which allows us to learn endless amounts of subjects and skills rather quickly, because we have the ability to say that this thing basically works like this other thing, thereby casting our understanding of the new in a familiar context.

Analogy is a broad and profound topic that is far beyond the scope of this book. It is mentioned here only to make you aware of its most basic concept, as it is encountered every day, in every culture, language, and country on the planet, and sometimes, merely being aware of a concept opens up unforeseen connections in your mind, (or, to be cheeky, new analogies.)

Keep in mind that the differences between a metaphor, a simile, and an analogy are sometimes quite subtle, and many people find their distinctions confusing even after explanation, so here are some examples to try and help clear things up for you. Remember, an analogy is drawing a comparison to something else in order to help someone understand the first by the similarities of the last.

Examples:

        "The *heart* is the body's *pump*."

        "The *rat race* of life is often overwhelming."

        "Green is to go as red is to stop."

        "Day is to humans what night is to bats."

        "What a wolf is to a bison, a cat is to a dog."

With these explanations and examples, you should now have at least a basic idea of some of the different parts of speech we encounter every day, as well as how and why they are used. If you're still unsure about the difference, as with everything in life, practice makes perfect. Come back to this section or do a simple internet search for more examples that may help clarify the subjects for you.

Idioms

Like figures of speech, there are far too many idioms in the English language to be able to list in this text, but that doesn't mean we can't explore them a little and shed some light on how they may or may not help your writing skills.

So what exactly is an idiom?

Most dictionaries define the word along the lines of: a word, or group of words, that express a meaning that is not the defined meaning of the words being used.

In essence, an idiom's meaning is *figurative* versus being *literal*.

For example:

"Acing the test was a piece of cake."

Literally, the sentence makes no sense whatsoever, and that's why a lot of non-native English speakers trying to learn the language often have difficulty understanding the meaning of idioms without the help of a native speaker or idiom dictionary.

Other examples include:

"It's *pouring buckets* outside."

"The old man *kicked the bucket* last night."

"This way we get *the best of both worlds*."

"*Speak of the devil*!"

"We failed to *see eye to eye*."

"It happens only *once in a blue moon*."
"It *cost me an arm and a leg*."
"It did nothing but *add insult to injury*."

As previously stated, there are more idioms than can be listed in this text, and there are new ones being added to the language all the time. Idioms are a living, breathing thing, just like languages themselves.

There are some things to be aware of when it comes to idioms, however:

#1: Idioms should not be confused with other common, (and previously covered), figures of speech such as the metaphor, which makes implicit comparisons, or the simile, which makes explicit comparisons, or with the hyperbole, which emphasizes a meaning through exaggeration.

#2: Idioms should also not be confused with proverbs, which are used to express a perceived piece of wisdom based on experience. An example of proverbs that could easily be mistaken for idioms include:

"Ignorance is bliss."
"You can catch more flies with honey than with vinegar."
"You can lead a horse to water, but you can't make it drink."

"Those who live in glass houses shouldn't throw stones."

Once again, like idioms, there are far too many proverbs in the English language to be able to list in this text.

#3: Idioms are rarely, if ever, capable of being translated into another language. If fact, they can rarely even be properly explained in a different language.

#4: There are differences between idioms in American English and British English. However, the meaning of the idiom is usually either the same, or very close in essence.

For example:
   American: "Skeletons in the closet."
   British: "Skeletons in the cupboard."

   American: "Knock on wood."
   British: "Touch wood."

   American: "See the forest for the trees."
   British: "See the wood for the trees."

#5: Idioms are useful devices to convey meaning to another person, but beware, as with many figures of speech, using them in formal contexts is often discouraged, and sometimes even frowned upon to the point of dismissal.

For your own good, use them with care.

<u>Voices. Are Some Better Than Others?</u>

In many grammar books and courses, one often comes across statements that urge a writer to try and avoid using the "passive voice" and instead focus on using the "active voice". So, what's the difference, anyway? Should you listen to this advice, or is it merely an opinion which, over time, has come to be understood as truth?

Let's first describe what a *voice* is in grammatical terms.

In English, there are two "grammatical voices," the active voice, and the passive voice. The "voice" itself refers to the verb of the sentence, and it describes the verb's action, (commonly referred to as its "state"), in relation to its subject and/or object.

Essentially, if the verb is doing something, then the sentence is said to be in the active voice.

Example 1: David drove through the fence.

Here, the verb "to drive" is in the active voice as it is responsible for portraying the action of the sentence. He *drove* through it.

Example 2: The fence was driven through by David.

Though a little awkward, this sentence is a perfect example of the "passive voice". Here, "the fence" was "driven through", the verb *happened* to the subject; therefore, the subject is responsible for conveying the action of the sentence. The verb is said to be *passive*.

To someone who isn't well versed or very interested in grammar, this subject can seem a little contrived and even a little overwhelming at first, but with just a little bit of practice you'll be able to spot the difference in anything you read.

> If the verb is what the subject *does*, it's active.
> If the action happens *to* the subject, it's passive.

Now, with that defined, let's take a look at why there are arguments for and against using one or the other, and why you should or shouldn't care.

The reality is that all writers use the passive voice, (even its critics), because the passive voice is used to emphasize what's happening to the subject of the sentence, and also to place other nouns other than the main figure in a subject position.

The point is that at the end of the day there isn't a rule that exists that says you should use one over the other, it's only a matter of opinion, and your usage of either should depend on the situation and what you're trying to convey with your writing. For example, if you're writing a client's quote, dominating your paragraphs with active verbs will help you come across as confident and determined, and the use of the passive voice can be used to emphasize certain characteristics or experience you may have.

On the other hand, a social media post has far less constraints, or even a need to come across one way or another. The idea of this section is only to make you aware that these two forms exist and they can, in certain situations, give your writing the extra punch you want in order to make an impression.

A note:

If this subject is still a little foggy, perhaps the discussion on verbs in the Parts Of Speech section of this book, (**p. 139**), may offer you a little more clarity.

<u>Don't Over Explain</u>

Let's start with an example:

"I took my brown and black cat, named Jag, to the vet on 42nd and 123rd street, right next to the liquor store where there always seems to be some homeless people hanging out and sometimes asking for money, because he was acting kind of weird and just wasn't his regular self, but when I got there I realized that in my rush to get there I'd forgotten my wallet, so Trudy, that's the receptionist's name, said that because I was a regular customer I could come back and pay the next day. So the doctor took a look at Jag and realized that he'd eaten a rubber band from like, I don't know where he got it, but anyway it was a big red one, and so they needed to perform surgery to remove it from his stomach. I'm so happy I got him there on time. Now I just owe the doc $1,500. Crazy cats, why do we love them so much?"

First off, a sentence like the one you see above, which jumps around from subject to subject and only uses commas to do it is what's called a *run on sentence*, and unless you're writing a novel and trying to display your skills at stream of consciousness or some other creative application, it is heavily frowned upon. There isn't anything inherently wrong with it; as in, it technically isn't grammatically incorrect, but it is a completely undirected mess.

There is no need to convey every piece of information to your recipient. In the case of our, (unfortunately not-so-contrived), example, the paragraph is loaded with unnecessary information that adds absolutely no value to the overall message the writer is trying to transmit. All he or she is really trying to say is:

My cat was acting strangely so I brought him to the vet. They ran a few tests and realized that he had a rubber band lodged in his stomach, so one operation, a lot worrying, and $1,500 later, he's back to himself again. Crazy cats! Why do we love them so much?

It's clear, concise, and conveys all the pertinent information relevant to the event.

The next time you find yourself describing an event, especially one in which you are emotionally invested, take a moment before sending it off to re-read it and put yourself in the shoes of your recipient. Is there a lot of unnecessary information included that does nothing more than obscure the facts?

Generalizing Is, Generally, A Bad Idea

Unless you're from a different planet, you should know that generalities relating to literally any possible subject relevant to human beings are rarely, if ever, accurate — except for this one.

It will benefit you greatly to avoid generalities in your writing, as, often, you're not aware of your recipient's background or history, and a generality can easily cause offense and/or make you seem less insightful than you'd like to portray.

Avoid, at all costs, if nothing else, stating things like: "Everybody knows", "It's common sense", or, "It's obvious that".

The truth of the world we live in is that, indeed, not everybody knows anything, there is no such thing as common sense, and things are rarely as obvious as you'd like to think they are.

Do yourself a favor and avoid using generalities like these. Rephrase what you want to say and try to specify it without relying on heuristics.

<u>Incomplete Thoughts</u>

Imagine yourself in a conversation:

"What's one thing you wish you'd done?" you ask your friend.

"I always wanted to speak French, but i never had the time," she replies.

"I know, right?" you say.
"It's like a warp zone," she says.

Now, this may be fine for a conversation because there are more factors at work than just the words that are involved in setting the context for the exchange, such as tone of voice, facial expressions, hand movements, body language, etc.

Writing, on the other hand, relies solely on the words to set the context for the meaning of the sentences, and as such, writers need to tread a fine line between expressing themselves clearly, avoiding the urge to over-explain, and simultaneously saying enough to prevent too much ambiguity from creeping into the reader's mind.

Of course, we may be able to infer the meaning of the conversation above, which is perfectly fine, and perhaps even preferable in a fiction novel. However, how much inference do you want the reader to be responsible for in your advertisement, your blog post, your code comments, or your sales contract? Preferably, almost, to absolutely, none, zero, nil. You want these sorts of documents to be as clear and unambiguous as possible, so that no inference can be the cause of confusion on the reader's part. It is *your* responsibility as the writer to ensure that as little ambiguity as possible is present where it really is to your advantage to avoid confusion.

"What's one thing you wish you'd done *earlier in your life?*" you ask your friend.

"I always wanted to speak French, but i never had the time *to sit down and really study it*," she replies.

"I know *exactly what you mean*, ~~right~~ *time just flies by, doesn't it?*" you say.

"It's like *we are living in* a warp zone *sometimes*," she says.

<u>Match Expectations</u>

This concept has been touched on multiple times already, but it's so important it's worth mentioning explicitly.

Let's say you have a meeting scheduled with a client looking to sign on with your company for a long term contract. Since you're meeting the CEO of this fake multi-national company, should you follow conventions and show up wearing the proper business attire, or should you opt to try and make a lasting impression by wearing surfer shorts and flip flops?

The first option will, one hundred percent, help you land that contract. The second one will, one hundred percent, insult your client, cause you to lose the contract, and miss out on additional business in the process for being so disrespectful.

This same concept of respect applies to your writing. If you're posting on social media for your friends to see, then there aren't really many constraints involved about the style or substance of what you're posting. (Usually). If you're writing an email to your employer, however, or submitting an application for admission to a networking organization, then some, (sometimes a lot), of consideration on your part will go a very long way to helping you succeed in your endeavor.

Additionally, on the subject of good social form, let's imagine you're signing a going away card for a fellow employee who is leaving the company, and your co-workers are writing things like: "Wish you the best of luck in the future! Hope to hear from you soon!" and "We had a great time! Congrats and sad to see you go!" and you come along and write something along the lines of: "I will miss the felicitation you brought with you every day. I wish you the best of luck in your peregrinations upon the globe and aspire to auscultate where you find yourself in the future." What do you think the recipient of the card will think when he/she reads what you wrote?

If you're hoping for something along the lines of: "Wow. What an extremely intelligent individual he/she is", well, sorry, friend, but that's highly unlikely. Far more likely is that they'll think you're a pretentious jerk.

Do yourself a favor when it comes to communicating with other people and *match expectations*.

<u>Colloquialisms</u>

Colloquialism is a formal word for slang, and yes, that in itself is rather ironic. The most important thing to understand about slang is that it is often a *regional* phenomenon, meaning that just because you and the people around you, in your city, or in your country, know the meaning of the word you're using, it shouldn't be assumed that its definition is known or can even be ascertained outside of those limits. Typically, slang words are used in casual oral conversations or other informal communications where the parties involved are familiar with the jargon being used.

It's important to be aware of when you're about to write a slang word, and then consider if its use is wise given the circumstances of the communication. If you're writing to a friend or posting on social media, then there shouldn't be much concern. If you're writing an instructional text or something like that, then maybe you should take a moment to consider using the accepted, dictionary defined word.

<u>Ambiguity</u>

We've already touched on the perils of ambiguity in this text, but it's a subject that deserves formal exploration as it can be useful to you in various ways, and especially in your every day communications.

Ambiguity is broadly defined as a sentence for which multiple, (two or more), meanings are plausible. However, it's important to understand that ambiguity isn't an evil. In fact, ambiguity can be leveraged and used to extraordinary effect in literary fiction, (and also in films), in order to layer the story and heighten its impact on the reader or viewer.

The trouble with ambiguity arises when it happens unintentionally. If you're trying to be as clear as possible, the presence of ambiguity in your writing presents itself to the reader as uncertainty, and your intended meaning is difficult or impossible to determine. If you've ever read an email or letter and asked yourself, "So, what are they saying? What do they mean? Is it this, or that?", then you've stared ambiguity in the face and might even have felt a fair level of frustration with the author.

The subject of ambiguity is a broad and intensive one that spans the fields of linguistics, literature, mathematics, philosophy, history, and more.

Our purpose here comes back to what has already been stated: make sure that you are being clear with what you're trying to convey. This comes down to a few linguistics concepts called: lexical ambiguity, semantic ambiguity, and vagueness, which are far beyond the scope of this book.

For your every day use, if you are not purposefully trying to be ambiguous, then the advice is to use the correct words to convey your meanings and to be precise with your descriptions.

<u>Section 3:</u>

How do I do what needs to be done?

This section moves beyond mere stylistic suggestions and into best practices one should probably always follow while writing. Unlike the previous section, these are often rather hard rules when it comes to writing in English.

<u>Contractions</u>

"It's a contraction," they say.
"Right," you say, shrugging. "A contraction."

So what exactly is a contraction?
A contraction is formed by combining, (literally, shortening), two words into one. So:

It is, becomes, It's.
Can not, becomes, can't.
Does not, becomes, doesn't.
Is not, becomes, isn't.
Would not, becomes, wouldn't.
They are, becomes, they're.
Have not, becomes, haven't.
Do not, becomes, don't.
Will not, becomes, won't.
Could have, becomes, could've.
Would have, becomes, would've.
Etc...

Quite naturally, in grammar, there are rules to follow; albeit, quite simple rules in this case:

#1: Avoid writing things like: *If I'd've known about it, I wouldn't've gone to the dance with him!* The problem with this sentence, if it isn't obvious, is the overuse of apostrophes. Instead of saying *I'd've* and *wouldn't've*, you really should chose a single contraction and write out the other word in the name of clarity and just a general good use of the English language.

If I would have known about it, I would not have gone to the dance with him!

If I'd have known about it, I wouldn't have gone to the dance with him!

If I would've known about it, I wouldn't have gone to the dance with him!

#2: Don't confuse *it's* and *you're*, the contractions of "it is" and "you are", with the possessive pronouns, *its* and *your*. (see pronouns in parts of speech **p.133**)

#3: Do not misspell the contractions involving the verb "have", as in could've, would've, should've, etc, with the *preposition* "of", as in could'of, would'of, should'of.

This error occurs because of the way people speak. When we say "Could've", we pronounce it as "Could'of"; however, in the written word, "Could'of," (and its variants), makes no sense whatsoever in any context.

This single error could cost you all of your credibility in an otherwise grammatically sound letter.

AVOID THIS ERROR AT ALL COSTS!

<u>A note:</u>

For more information on the preposition "of", see prepositions in, parts of speech section (**p. 121**)

<u>Forming Possessives</u>

Continuing on from our exploration of contractions, (and in order to support its understanding), let's now have a look at possessives.

Avoiding an in depth examination of the grammatical considerations, (and in depth it does get), a possessive is exactly what it sounds like: It *belongs* to something.

So what is "it" and "what" does it belong to? Well . . .

In the "contraction" section, you were warned against misusing the contraction "it's" for the possessive pronoun"its".

The best way to remember the difference between "it's" and "its", is if you cannot say "it is", then you're looking for "its".

Example:
    The dog loves to run after *its* ball.
Here, *its* is used because the ball *belongs* to the dog.

    The tree is losing *its* leaves.
Again, *its* is used because leaves *belongs* to the tree.

Alternatively:
    The dog can't catch the ball it's after.

Here, *it's* is used because the dog cannot catch the ball *it is* after.

Things begin to change when forming possessives using nouns instead of pronouns, however.

Example:

      The *tree's* leaves are falling from *its* branches. Here we are forming two possessives. The first is *tree's*, because the leaves *belong* to the tree, and the second is *its*, because the branches belong to *it*, a pronoun for the tree.

Here are a few simple tips and tricks for forming possessives in your writing:

      The main thing to remember is the difference between *singular nouns* and *plural nouns*.

#1: To form the possessive of a singular noun, whether it ends with an "s" or not, you simply add an 's, (apostrophe s), at the end of the noun.

Example:

      Kelly's ball.
      The boss's keys.
      The lady's purse.
      Alex Stevens's license plate number begins with a letter.

#2: To form the possessive of a plural noun, you simply add an apostrophe and omit the s.

Example:

    The girls' teacher.
    It's a three hours' drive to my house.
    The employees' refused to sign the new contract.
    The Wagners' boat was stolen last night.

Things to remember:

    Take care to avoid pluralizing a singular noun when a possessive is what's called for.

Example:

    The *buildings* lights, should be: The building's lights.
    The *cities* parks, should be: The city's parks.
    The *guys* car, should be: The guy's car.
    The *benches* legs, should be: The bench's legs.

In addition to the above advice, and as per our previous discussion, it's worthwhile to remember the difference between "it's" and "its", and that the possessive personal pronouns "theirs", "his", "hers", "ours", and "yours" are the same as "its" and therefore require no apostrophe or apostrophe s.

<u>Double Negatives</u>

Examples of double negatives are as follows:

> "I don't know no one name Evan."
> "I have never said nothing like that."
> "I never went nowhere yesterday."
> "I didn't not finish school."

There is a deep and sometimes passionate debate about the validity of double negatives in the English language. Technically, there is nothing wrong with them, and, in fact, the clauses they appear in can be classified as either positive or negative. They are mentioned here, however, only to make you aware that using double negatives in any sort of formal context will most likely discredit your letter.

Carefully consider rewriting your sentence if you're unsure about how it will be perceived by the recipient.

> "I don't know anyone named Evan."
> "I've never said anything like that."
> "I didn't go anywhere yesterday."
> "I did finish school."

Capitalization

In English, the rules for the capitalization of words are fairly straight-forward and easy to understand compared to languages like German, where the first word following a period is capitalized, and also every noun, whether proper or not, within the sentence. But since this is a text about the English language, let's have a look at its rules.

#1: Capitalize the first word of every sentence.

#2: Capitalize proper nouns, like: Keith, Shelley, Texas, Germany, Toronto, Utah.

#3: Capitalize the singular first-person pronoun "I", as well as all of its contractions: "I'll", "I'd", "I'm".

#4: The first word in a title is usually capitalized. Also, some titles capitalize the first letter of every word for emphasis. That is acceptable.

#5: Especially when writing an email, writing something in ALL CAPS is a convention that is usually interpreted by the recipient as you screaming at them. Unless you mean to be screaming at your fellow interlocutor, you should avoid doing it.

And that's about it for the every day use of capitalization. The "rules" are really more of conventions and long held opinions, but using them accordingly will help you be clear and concise in your writing.

Do I Add An -*er* Or Use *More* Before An Adjective?

This rule concerns *comparative adjectives,* which are defined as adjectives that denote a greater intensity of one of two things, as well as *superlative adjectives,* which are adjectives that express *the greatest intensity* of one of two things. As with many grammatical rules, there isn't *really* a definite rule for this one. It's more a matter of style and convention than anything else, a rule of thumb, in idiomatic terms.

This "rule" is based on syllables.
Not quite sure what syllables are?
Well, let's have a quick look at them first.

As with most linguistics related subjects, this is one which you can follow down the rabbit hole if you'd like, but its full exploration is beyond the scope of our purpose here. At its most basic definition, a syllable is a *phonological*, (speech sound), unit of organization.

For example, the name, David, is composed of 2 syllables: *Da* and *vid.*

Examples:

Sound = one-syllable word (called *monosyllabic*)

Printer = two-syllable word (called *disyllable*)

Umbrella = three-syllable word (called *trisyllable*)

Execution = four-syllable word (called *polysyllable* and refers to any word with more than one syllable)

As previously stated, this subject is very broad and includes some very explicit rules, but for our purpose the above explanation will have to do. Say the words out loud and count the syllables.

Sound.
Prin - ter.
Um - brell - a.
Ex - e - cu - tion.

Now, when it comes to comparative adjectives, the rule of thumb is as follows:

For one-syllable comparative adjectives, the majority of words will add an *-er* to the end, and for polysyllabic comparative adjectives, the word *more* is used.

Examples of monosyllabic adjectives:
Big = "Mine is *bigger* than his."
Clear = "The picture is much *clearer* now."
High = "I ended up going *higher* than she did."
Dark = "Then things became *darker*."

Examples of polysyllabic adjectives:

> Curious = "I became a lot *more* curious about the case."
> Nervous = "He just became *more* and *more* nervous as the day went on."
> Perfect = "She wants it *more* perfect than what you say it already is."
> Difficult = "Learning an Asian language is *more* difficult than learning a Latin tongue."

When it comes to superlative adjectives, the rule of thumb is essentially the same:

For one-syllable superlative adjectives, the majority of words will add an -*est* to the end, and for polysyllabic superlative adjectives, the word *most* is used.

** Remember, all a "superlative adjective" really means is that you want to express the *most intensity*, you're no longer increasing the intensity, as in the comparative adjective, you're at the limit of intensity.

Examples of monosyllabic adjectives:

> Big = "Mine is the *biggest*."
> Clear = "That's the *clearest* picture I've seen."
> High = "I was *highest* on the mountain."
> Dark = "Things are at their *darkest*."

Examples of polysyllabic adjectives:

> Curious = "That's when I became *most* curious about the case."
>
> Nervous = "He was the *most* nervous of everyone there."
>
> Perfect = "She wants it to be the *most* perfect painting she's ever produced."
>
> Difficult = "Asian languages are the *most* difficult of all languages to learn."

Naturally, there are exceptions, and these exceptions are called *irregular adjectives,* and they function the same way as irregular verbs do, (**p. 151**). These adjectives don't form comparative and superlative adjectives like the examples above. Instead, the entire word changes depending on its usage.

Examples:

Adjective	Comparative	Superlative
Little	Less	Least
Bad	Worse	Worst
Much	More	Most

In addition to these, the following adjectives **do not have comparative and superlative forms:**

Dead, Fatal, Right, Unique, Blind, Left, Vertical, Wrong, Universal, Final.

How do I make words plural?

In English, the plural form of nouns seems straight-forward: you just add an "s" at the end. The reality, however, is slightly different, because like the vast majority of rules in grammar, there are exceptions.

Regular plurals are nouns to which adding "-es" or "s" is all that is necessary to make the noun plural.

Examples:
> Dog = Dogs
> Dish = Dishes
> Truck = Trucks
> Job = Jobs

But keep these exceptions in mind:

#1: Some nouns that end with an "o" require an "-es" to be added rather than just an "s".
> Example: volcano = volcanoes

#2: Some nouns that end with a "y" require an "-ies" to be added rather than just an "s".
> Example: cherry = cherries

#3: Some nouns are called, *near-regular plurals*, and these require the noun to change in order to form a plural.

Examples:
>Leaf = Leaves
>Knife = Knives
>Life = Lives

Note: there are also exceptions to these. Certain nouns can do both:

>Elf = Elfs or Elves
>Turf = Turfs or Turves
>Dwarf = Dwarfs or Dwarves

#4: Some nouns are called, *irregular plurals*, and they are spelled exactly the same way whether they are singular or plural.

Examples:
>Cod
>Deer
>Moose
>Shrimp
>Spacecraft
>Cherokee
>People

#5: Some nouns are called, *mutated plurals*, and these require the changing of the vowel sound in order to form the plural.

Examples:

> Goose = Geese
> Foot = Feet
> Mouse = Mice
> Tooth = Teeth
> Man = Men
> Woman = Women

<u>Neither, Nor. Either, Or</u>

These are very common errors, and particular care should be taken to ensure that these are correct when writing any sort of formal letter.

#1: If you use the word either, use or:
Example: "Take *either* this one, *or* that one."

#2: If you use the word neither, use nor:
Example: "You can have *neither* this one, *nor* that one."

The common error here happens most often with the word "neither", as many people follow it with the word "or".

A simple mnemonic for it is: **Neither takes an N, so use nor.**

<u>Punctuation</u>

There are many forms of punctuation available in the English language. Some are basic and intuitive, while others are not. This text will not cover all punctuations; namely, we will skip the colon, the semicolon, the hyphen, the dash, the square brackets, ellipsis points, the slash, as well as the use of italics and underlining. Since this book's primary goal is the enhancement of your writing/communication skills to an intermediate level, we will have a look at only the most common punctuation marks, and only with a very high level overview at that.

Let's get started.

#1: The Period:

We start with the period, the easiest and most intuitive of all the punctuation marks. As anyone who's ever written a sentence knows, sentences other than questions or exclamations always end with a period. If they do not, then you've introduced confusion and ambiguity into your message and risk a failure in properly conveying your message.

As simple as the period is, however, there are a few things you should be aware of.

-First, you should take care not to use a period where a comma is called for.

Example:

> Incorrect: "I lost my dog in the park yesterday. Of all places."

> Correct: "I lost my dog in the park yesterday, of all places."

-Secondly, in a freestanding parenthesized or quoted sentence, the period is always placed inside of these marks, ***not on the outside***.

Examples:

> Incorrect: (This is a freestanding parenthesized sentence).

> Correct: (This is a freestanding parenthesized sentence.)

> Incorrect: "But he just told me it wasn't true".

> Correct: "But he just told me it wasn't true."

The exception to this is if a sentence ends with a parenthesized abbreviation, then the period goes before and after the final parenthesis.

Example:

> "Caesar was assassinated on the Ides Of March, (March 15th, 44 B.C.)."

#2: The Exclamation Point:

The exclamation point is used to denote amazement, surprise, or anger. It is also an all-too-common target for punctual abuse! Inexperienced writers try to use it in order to try and infuse weakly structured and mundane sentences with more energy or drama than they warrant! The best advice a new or inexperienced writer can receive is to use the exclamation point sparingly! It can be used after interjections, (see parts of speech section **p. 117**), like: Ouch! Yikes! Jeez! Huh! It can also be used in dialogue, like: "I'm using an exclamation point!" Using it for anything more than short, declarative sentences will end up having the opposite effect than the one you seek in your writing.

Got it?

Got it!

#3: The Question Mark:

One would think that the use of the question mark comes as naturally as the period and exclamation point, but one may be surprised when trying to use it extensively to find that all sorts of uncertainties begin to creep up out of nowhere. Should I use one here, or am I supposed to end this sentence with a period? How can anyone know this stuff for sure? How can anyone know anything for sure? Is life even . . . real?

Fear not, for there are guidelines to help you out.

-A question mark should be placed at the end of a *direct question*.

Example: "What's your name?"

Be diligent, however, because the use of a question mark can easily be cast into doubt when using it with dialogue or a train of thought.

Example: "What's you name?" she said.
Example: What's his name? she wondered.

-A PERIOD should be used at the end of an *indirect question*.

Example:

"She asked if she could borrow the car."
"He was wondering if you'd be home for dinner."
"She's always asking why I do these things."

In this vein, also beware of the fact that sometimes an indirect question can be expressed by a single word. This is often the example that confuses inexperienced

writers. These are still indirect questions and they must
be punctuated with a period.

Example:
> "I had my keys in my pocket and now they're
> gone, but the question is where."

> "She asked her and she mumbled some excuses,
> but she still wouldn't tell her why."

> "I need to get him a birthday gift he'll like, but I
> don't know what to get him."

-Many formal requests, although written in the form of
a question, are still punctuated with a period.

Example:
> "Could you please respond by Saturday."
> "Would you please complete the form and return
> it to the attendant."

#4: Quotation Marks:
Quotation marks are used to show the reader
that someone other than the writer wrote or said the
words they contain.

Example:
> And then Shelley said, "What are you, a wimp?"

> In the words of Napoleon, "Soldiers will fight long and hard for a bit of ribbon."

Quotation marks are also used in fiction in order to denote dialogue between characters, thereby separating the narration, the actions, and the speech.

Example:

> "Where is your mother?" she asked, waging a finger in the air.
> "I don't know," said the little boy.

In addition to these uses, quotation marks are also often used to convey a sense of sarcasm in a sentence.

Example:

> "Our "illustrious mayor" has said that he plans to clean up the streets."

> "She sent me home because she said I wasn't "proper" in my speech."

#5: The Parentheses:

Parentheses are used to add a layer of extra information into an already complete sentence. Usually, the information contained within parentheses is of less importance than what is in the rest of the sentence, but does *relate directly* to the sentence's existing content.

Example:

> "She could get done, (so she claimed), in less than a week."

> "He likes the word polychromatic, (an adjective), which means to exhibit a variety of colors."

#6: The Comma:

Finally, we have arrived at the comma, by far the most complex and most commonly misused punctuation mark in the every day writings of the English language. The danger of exploring the comma is the depth to which we can plunge, thereby obscuring the need, the absolute necessity for you, the budding writer, to understand the comma and its critical role in the English language. Thus, we will here give a high level overview of how and when, and when not to use our poorly understood friend, the comma.

#1: Always use a comma after an address.

Example:

> Dear Mr. Forrester,

#2: Always use a comma when signing off a letter.

Examples:

> Sincerely, Thomas

Thank you, Management
Until next time, Karen

#3: Always use a comma after a *transitional phrase*.

Examples:
In fact,
However,
Furthermore,

<u>A note:</u> Do not confuse a transitional phrase with a conjunction. (see parts of speech section **p. 118** , as well as transitions **p. 112**)

#4: Always use a comma when using two consecutive adjectives to modify a noun.

Examples:
"We then entered the *cold, dark* room."
"I mounted the *big, muscular* horse all on my own."

#5: Always use a comma after each element of a series of three or more items.

Examples:
"I need a paintbrush, a stool, and an easel."
"He said he brought her sailing, swimming, and sunbathing."

#6: Always use a comma when writing the date.

Example:
"I was born on Tuesday, November 24th, 1980."

#7: Always use a comma between a city and a country.

Example:
"We visited him in Edmonton, Canada."

Here you have the most basic rules of the comma, but as was previously stated, there are more, (many, many more), that, should you be so inclined, you can learn all about in an exhaustive and authoritative book of grammar.

Rest assured, however, that what we have here described will go a long way to ensuring your writing is clearly expressed and concise in its meaning.

Tip: If you need to remind yourself of how periods and quotation marks are to be properly used, grab the nearest novel and have a gander at the dialogue.

<u>Bastard Enumeration</u>

That's right, there is a thing called Bastard Enumeration in grammar, and it falls under the purview of what's known as, *faulty parallelism*. It is mentioned here because it is a sore point to many a grammar enthusiast, and probably why it was named bastard enumeration in a fit of rage and disgust by Henry Watson Fowler, a literary scholar and gentleman.

The idea here refers to having two, or three, or more elements in a sentence and treating them as if they are equal, when they in fact are not.

Examples are often the best teachers.

#1: "I visited the Louvre, the Eiffel Tower, and I wanted to see Versailles."

The issue in this first example is that the writer has stated they he/she HAS visited two location, but then abruptly states that he/she WANTS to visit another. The sentence is written as though it were a standard a,b, and c list, but it is not.

#2: "I love apples, bananas, and birds."

A less striking example, to be sure, but nonetheless considered incorrect by the strict grammar aficionado. If you name two fruits, you best name a third just to keep things consistent. Birds are not fruit!

#3: "I walked, swam, and felt like crap all day."

Here we have an action verb, an action verb, and a linking verb leading to an adjective. There is a desperate, burning desire to have things neat and tidy among grammar fanatics, and when they come across something like this, it's often enough to make some of them pull their hair out.

The true lesson here, though, is that you *don't always know whom you're writing to*. Some people may be warehouse managers or delivery drivers by day, but by night they take pleasure, (yes, some do), in the study of grammar and all of its wonderful complexities. Thus, beware, for some people, a bastard enumeration is crossing the line, and often equivalent to a declaration of war.

Yes, of course I'm exaggerating.
But seriously, don't do this.

Choosing Between Who, That, And Which

This is a common source of confusion for writers, and for our purpose we'll avoid diving into the sometimes complex rules of grammar that guide their proper usage, and instead give you some loose guidelines that should help you make a decision on which word to use in your text.

#1: If you are referring to things, use *Which*.
> "*Which* did you bring, the coffee or the tea?"
> "He came from town, *which* is that way."

#2: If you are referring to people, use *Who*.
> "*Who* is that man?"
> "He said it came from Derek, but I don't know *who* that is."

#3: If you are referring to things or, informally, to people, use *That*.
> "I saw the man driving *that* car last night."
> "They're the people *that* gave us those flyers."

A note: Even though it's stated that you can use *That* when referring informally to people, you will never err by using *Who,* even in informal situations.

He, She, Or They?

Well, ladies and gentlemen and, others, what we have here is a sore point. The problem is that in English, there are **no personal pronouns,** (specifically, third person *singular* pronouns: his, hers, he, she, etc.), that *can* refer to a person without ascribing either a male or female gender to them. (for pronouns, see parts of speech, **p. 133**).

Over the years, people have attempted solutions, the most common of which, (and one that is used in this book), is to simply use both, as in: "He/She said that happened yesterday." This approach is grammatically correct and mostly unobtrusive as long as there is no need for you to continually refer to "he/she" repeatedly throughout the text.

Other people, (some wisecrackers, some grammar devotees would say), decided that instead of using "he/she", they could simply use the plural pronouns: they, their, them, etc. From an intuitive standpoint, this seems to make sense as it eliminates the gender tag; however, some people object to the use of a *plural* pronoun that refers back to a *singular* pronoun on the basis that it is **grammatically incorrect.** Some defenders of the practice point to the fact that this sort of thing was a common practice in English a few hundred years ago, and it is now, today, an extremely common practice that goes unnoticed by most, but their opponents point out that it is no longer "a few hundred years ago," nor does the frequency of its current use change the fact that it is **incorrect**.

Few subjects in grammar are so hotly debated, and as far as whether you should use it or not is, really, up to you. I personally side with the fact that it is in every way incorrect and should not be used. However, you are free to choose your side, if any, and write from thence.

Ain't Just Ain't A Word, Except . . .

It is one hundred percent true; ain't is not an accepted English word.

It's amazing, really, because it's been in popular use for a very long time, something like three hundred plus years, and it can be considered grammatically correct, and yet, year after year it is staunchly refused entry into the dictionary. Whatevs, OMG, and Bromance are all new additions to the Oxford dictionary, but not ain't.

Why is that?

Well, it's difficult to tell. Its original grammatical value was as a contraction of *am not* as in "I am not sure." "I ain't sure," therefore should be a straightforward entry into the dictionary, but it later came into popular usage to mean *are not* and *is not,* (instead of aren't and isn't), and was, therefore, banned from what was, and still is, considered to be correct and proper English.

That being said, the word "ain't" is extremely common in modern English, (especially "American" English), and appears everywhere from mainstream entertainment to the casual conversations of people from all social, educational, and financial levels.

In writing, however, it is ***not*** acceptable to use ain't in anything that is considered formal. Do not use it to communicate with anyone with which you have a professional relationship. If you're posting on social media or sending an email to a friend, then feel free to use it with reckless abandon.

<u>Using Un vs. Dis vs. Mis</u>

Disinterested, or uninterested? Misinformed, or uninformed? Disorganized, or unorganized? This last one is probably the easiest of the three examples to differentiate between, but the core of this problem is actually quite complicated and rather difficult to answer.

There are certain words that are intuitive, but others, such as disinterested or uninterested aren't always so cut and dry. (Be sure, however, there is a difference between the two.) The best advice in this case is to check your dictionary when the word to use isn't clear. Before using it, make sure it exists and means what you intend it to mean before using it.

You'd be surprised by how many sentences are plagued, day after day, by the misuse of unused words.

The Paragraph And The Transition

In English, the organization of your writing into paragraph form is not strictly necessary, but it is strongly recommended, especially in formal circumstances. Paying attention to the physical layout of your text can add a tremendous amount of clarity to your ideas. It can also provide extra impact to the messages you're conveying, and depending on the situation, it can even become part of the writing or story itself.

There is, however, as with most facets of writing in English, often a passionate debate about how paragraphs should be used, when, and why. Public schools typically teach a generic form of layout that includes each paragraph having a "topic sentence" with "supporting sentences" following it that expand on the topic, and that is, generally, considered a proper way to lay out your thoughts and ideas in a concise way. However, forms of the paragraph and what's included and/or not is subject to change based on the type of writing that is being done, (i.e., journalism, fiction, essay, etc.)

In general, following the advice of keeping a "topic sentence" with "supporting sentences" is useful and correct. If you need further explanation on forming paragraphs, it's as easy as leafing through any book, like the one you're currently reading, and simply paying attention to how the paragraphs are structured, how the ideas that are related to one another are grouped together, and further explanation and/or additional information is grouped into additional paragraphs.

Also note that many style guides and school curriculums teach that paragraphs should generally be kept short and contain no more than 3 to 5 sentences, but this is merely opinion and not based on any concrete reason other than personal preference. There is nothing wrong with long paragraphs as long as the ideas flow in a clear and logical manner.

Much of writing, including much of, (but not all!), grammar is a matter of preference and/or opinion.

Now, this is all good and well, but there's still something missing. Paragraphs are good for organizing thoughts, but when grouped they can often make a text choppy, meaning the writing jumps around from one idea to the next in an abrupt and sometimes forceful manner. To help smooth out the transition from one idea to the next, from one paragraph to the next, you need to use something called exactly that: a *Transition.*

<u>Transitions</u>

Transitions provide a way to connect and change between different ideas in a way that is smooth and logical. It is what's responsible for much of the *flow* of your text, and when properly employed, it's what can take a good text and make it great. Transitions add that finishing polish that really makes a text stand out. While speaking, the vast majority of people use transitions without even realizing it, but when it comes to writing, ironically, their use can sometimes be a subtle and even intimidating prospect to attempt.

In English, transitions are employed between sentences, as well as between paragraphs, (usually to begin a new paragraph), and their role is to form bridges over which a reader can easily evolve from one sentence to the next, one idea or thought to the next, one point to the next, or one mood to the next.

<u>A note:</u> You can see examples of this throughout this or pretty much any other book you're willing to analyze.

In linguistics, there are four general categories of transitions, and as you'll see as you make your way through this book, these categories are very similar to other grammatical concepts we'll be exploring in the parts of speech section (**p. 116**).

#1: Coordinating Transition:

Coordinating transitions are used to display a relationship between elements that are of equal significance.

- To display similarity, use words like: and, also, in addition, furthermore, comparatively.
- To present an opposing point, use words like: but, however, yet, on the other hand, nevertheless.
- To reinforce a point, use words like: in other words, that is, meaning, to be sure.

#2: Subordinating Transitions:

Subordinating transitions are generally used to introduce things like lists, or examples.

- To introduce a series, use words like: first, second, third, firstly, secondly, thirdly, the first example, the second example, the third example, next, then, finally.
- To introduce an example, use words like: for instance, for example, particularly.
- To show a determinant, use words like: hence, thus, as a result, so, because.
- To arrive at a conclusion, use words like: in conclusion, finally, clearly.
- To move to a concession, use words like: of course, it's true that, to be sure, naturally.

#3: Temporal Transitions:

Temporal transitions are those that relate to time.

- For frequency, use words like: hourly, often, occasionally, sometimes, eventually.
- For duration, use words like: all along, for a time, a moment, briefly.
- For a particular time, use words like: right now, it used to be, in the past, in the future.

#4: Spatial Transitions:

Spatial transitions, as the name implies, deal with space and dimensions.

- For closeness, use words like: near, next to, beside.
- For distance, use words like: over there, beyond, away.
- For direction, use words like: up, down, sideway, across, right, left.

A note: In the parts of speech section (**p. 116**), many of the words used here will be redefined as prepositions, nouns, verbs, adjectives, adverbs, and conjunctions. Keep in mind that what we are concentrating on here is strictly the use of transitions, not the grammatical identity of the individual words. Make sure you understand the difference, because as you'll see again and again, when it comes to writing in English, the identity of the word you're using is often determined by _the role it is playing in a sentence_.

For now, simply disregard the identity of the words and instead concentrate on the concept of a transition because its proper use will go a long way toward making your writing shine above that of others who do not understand how to properly connect their ideas into a logical and concise form.

Section 4:

An Overview Of The Parts Of Speech:

The parts of speech are exactly what they sound like. They make up the bits and pieces from which sentences are constructed and strewn together to form wonderful worlds, meaningful messages, profound philosophies, and many other incredible feats that can only be achieved by the human mind.

As has been repeatedly stated, this text is not meant to be an authoritative exploration of English grammar; however, knowing at least the basics of grammar will help you communicate with other people in ways you never thought possible. A little understanding goes a long way toward meaningful connections of all kinds, and if you find yourself suddenly enamored with the concepts herein taught, you are therefore urged to stick your nose into a slightly more grammar intensive book and enjoy the powers it will impart to you.

The first lesson to learn is that there are 8 parts of speech. Yes, some are much easier to understand and use than others, but all of them are among some of the most wonderful and useful inventions of the human mind.

Enjoy!

#1: Interjections

Whoa! Ouch! Come on! Wow!
All of the above are interjections. They stand alone, expressing strong emotions, and having no grammatical relation to the rest of the sentence. In fact, they can be thought of as *intensifiers*, helping to emphasize the emotion of the upcoming sentence, but not grammatically modifying it in any way. If it was removed from the sentence, it wouldn't change the meaning one bit.

Whoa! What was that? vs. What was that?

When the interjection is expressing a strong emotion, like Argh! or Whoops!, use an exclamation point. On the other hand, if the interjection is expressing a milder emotion, like Well, or Huh, use a comma instead.

Also, use interjections with care. The overuse of them produces exactly the same effect as overusing the exclamation point. It's bad practice and makes for bad writing.

Onward!

#2: Conjunctions

Conjunctions are the cogs in the wheels of the English language. They are what allow for complex thoughts and descriptions to be linked together to form larger ideas and move, entertain, and/or inform the person reading them.

There are three main forms of the conjunction.

#1: The Coordinating Conjunction:

The coordinating conjunction is everywhere, in everything you read, have read, and will ever read. These are words that connect or link together similar sentence components.

There is a popular mnemonic device for remembering these:

> *fanboys: for, and, nor, but, or, yet, so*

#2: Correlative Conjunction:

We've seen the correlative conjunction before in our discussion about neither/nor and either/or. The important thing to remember about correlative conjunctions is that they cannot stand alone. If you use neither, you MUST use nor. If you use either, you MUST use or. Other correlative conjunction pairs include:

Both/and
Not only/also
Not only/but also

Example:

"Mr. Henry *not only* asked her to the dance, *but also* gave her a necklace to wear."

#3: The Subordinating Conjunction:

Unlike the coordinating conjunction, the subordinating conjunction links together sentence component that are not grammatically similar or equivalent. They join sentence elements only when one element depends on the other for meaning.

Example:

"After the rain, we went swimming."
"Since I had no money, I just stayed home."

These conjunctions include:

After, although, as in, as if, as long as, as much as, as soon as, assuming that, because, before, even though, how, if, in order that, in that, inasmuch as, now that, once, providing that, since, so long as, so that, than, that, though, unless, until, when, where, whenever, wherever, whether, while.

#4: Conjunctive Adverbs:

These words are *adverbs,* (**p. 125**)*,* that serve the purpose of a conjunction. These are the words most often used after a semicolon, and they are:

Moreover, however, therefore, thus, hence, consequently, furthermore, nevertheless, instead, then.

Debunking the myth:
Do you want to begin your sentence using a "but", or an "and", or a "yet", well, friend, go nuts, because there is absolutely nothing wrong with beginning a sentence with a conjunction. It is grammatically sound to proceed.

#3: Prepositions

Many texts try to introduce prepositions by stating that they link nouns and/or pronouns to other elements in a sentence, such as a verb or an adjective, and although such an explanation is correct, there is an easier way to digest this beast.

First, let's break down the word: Pre-position.

The basic definition is actually quite literal. A preposition is often used *before* a noun or pronoun and typically defines or expresses a spatial, temporal, or other relationship related to a position. Keep this idea of position in mind as you read through the list of common prepositions:

About, above, across, after, against, along, amid, among, around, as, at, before, behind, below, beneath, beside, between, beyond, by, concerning, despite, down, during, except, for, from, in, inside, including, into, like, of, off, on, onto, out, over, near, past, regarding, since, through, throughout, to, toward, under, underneath, until, unto, up, upon, while, with, within, without.

In addition to these, there are also compound prepositions which are formed by combining single word prepositions:

Across from, alongside of, ahead of, apart from, by means of, down by, down under, in case of, in favor of, in front of, in regard to, in spite of, inside of, on account of, regardless of, such as, together with.

Now, you'll probably be starting to notice that some of these words, (and you'll see it again with adverbs), are beginning to overlap. Weren't some of these conjunctions? Aren't some of these adverbs? And the answer to your question is, as stated in the previous section, it depends on their function within the sentence. How you use these words determines what their definition is. A little bit of practice is all it takes to begin clearing up the confusion.

Debunking Another Myth:
Is your sentence ending with a preposition, like "to", or "of", or "with"? Make no changes, friend, it's all perfectly correct and proper grammar. It is still grammatically sound to proceed.

#4: Adjectives

An adjective is a word that modifies a noun or pronoun by adding a *description* to it. Colors are a perfect example of adjectives.

> "Her eyes are *blue*."
> "The *red* curtains sway in the wind."
> "The *black* earth smells fresh."

Adjectives can usually appear either before or after the word it modifies, and it answers one of these three questions:
> What kind?
> Which one?
> How many?

Example:
> "It's the *big* house on the right."

Which house? The *BIG* one.
What kind? Big.

The ultimate role of an adjective is to provide certain characteristics to people, places, or things in order to help the reader visualize it in a precise way. They determine which thing, what kind of thing, and/or how many things there are.

****Articles:**

Articles are a special type of adjective and they contain precisely three words: **A, An, The.** Within this simple group of three words, there are two different types of articles.

The first, which refers to **A** and **An**, is called an *indefinite article* because it does not specify anything specific. It's *a* car, *a* lake, *an* umbrella. There is an easy way to determine how to chose between using **a** or **an** when you are writing. The rule of thumb is that if the word the article refers to, (ex: a car), does not begin with a *vowel sound*, then you use **A**. If, on the other hand, the word *does* begin with a vowel sound, (ex: an umbrella), then you do use **An**.

Naturally, there are some points of contention within the grammar community, like, for example, if one should write "a history" or "an history".

As usual, it comes down to a matter of preference and personal choice.

Now, the second article is called a *definite article* and it refers solely to the word **The**. As you can probably tell, it's called a definite article because it specifies a specific person, object, thing, idea, etc. It's *the* car, *the* lake, *the* umbrella.

Yes, **The** is the only definite article in the English language.

#5: Adverbs

The adverb is somewhat similar to a wildcard in the English language. It has powers not granted to any other type of speech component; namely, it has the ability to modify nearly any other word in a sentence including nouns, verbs, adjectives, and even other adverbs. As with any other powerful tool, however, an abuse of its powers will cause catastrophic results to your once innocent sentences.

Adverbs can be tricky to spot in a sentence when a writer isn't quite sure of their definition. The first broad definition is that adverbs very often, but not always, end with a -ly.

Example:
Safely, cautiously, joyfully, attentively.

Beware, however, because there are adjectives that also end with an -ly.

Example:
Timely, friendly, costly.

Given this possible confusion, the best way to identify an adverb is to ask if the word in question answers one of the following questions:

How? Where? When? Why? Under What Circumstance? How Much? To What Extent? How Often?

Example:
   Quite frankly, I'm feeling *rather* confused.

- In this example, the word "Quite" is an adverb that answers the question: How?
- The word "frankly" is an adverb that also answers the question: How? This adverb is also being modified by the adverb "Quite".
- The word "rather" is an adverb that answers the question: To What Extent?

As we've already mentioned in the section about conjunctions, (**p. 118**), there are conjunctive adverb, and they include words that connect two clauses, phrases, or sentences by indicating an additional thought. They are words like:

However, in addition, also, instead, likewise, furthermore, therefore, thus.

There are many, and these words can also serve other purposes within a sentence. Remember, the grammatical definition of a word comes down to what purpose it is serving in a sentence, therefore, one is bound to find the same word appearing in multiple parts of speech, but serving a different purpose within each one.

Tip: Download a dictionary app to your phone, tablet, or computer, and whenever you find yourself uncertain about which part of speech a word may be, simply look it up. Dictionaries, including physical ones, often list a word and all of its variations depending on which part of speech is being used.

Example:
> Word: Man
> Noun, plural, men.
> Adverb: Manly.
> Verb: manned, manning
> Interjection: Man!
> Verb phrases: Man up!
> Idioms: as one man, be one's own man, a man's man, man to man

In addition to this exploration of adverbs, it's necessary to mention that adverb, exactly like our previous discussion about adjectives (**p. 84**), also have comparative and superlative forms. Thus, when two items are being compared, you use the comparative, and when more than two items are being compared, you use the superlative form of an adverb.

Examples of adverbs ending in -ly:

Adverb	Comparative	Superlative
Proudly	More proudly	Most proudly
Safely	More safely	Most safely
Slowly	More slowly	Most slowly

Examples of monosyllable adverbs or adverbs ending only with a -y:

Adverb	Comparative	Superlative
Late	Later	Latest
High	Higher	Highest
Easy	Easier	Easiest

**Remember, some adjectives can also be adverbs. It depends on the purpose they are serving.

Examples of irregular adverbs, just like adjectives:

Adverb	Comparative	Superlative
Little	Less	Least

Adverb	Comparative	Superlative
Well	Better	Best
Much	More	Most

#6: Nouns

Nouns are, on the surface, one of the more intuitive parts of speech, because nouns name things. As simple as that is, however, there are a few different types of nouns, and the two over-arching types are ***Proper Nouns***, as in people's names, cities, countries, certain things and ideas, and these are *always* capitalized. The other type are called ***Common Nouns*** and these name classes or groups, for example, cat, forest, boulder.

Following from these two broad categories, nouns are further classified into several other categories. Here are a few you're likely to come into contact with on a daily basis:

#1: Collective Nouns:

These are nouns that specify many things but are considered singular. Examples of collective nouns are the words: *people, herd, family, swarm, troop.*

#2: Concrete Nouns:

Concrete Nouns name tangible, concrete things that we can experience with our five senses of sight, smell, taste, touch, and sound. They include almost everything around us, like: *table, chair, bed, linen, window, tree.*

#3: Abstract Nouns:

Abstract nouns name things that lie beyond our five senses of sight, smell, taste, touch, and sound. They name things like: *beliefs, philosophies, ideas, and qualities, among others.*

#4: Count Nouns:

Count nouns are nouns that can *always* be pluralized. In other words, they can be one thing, like a *hat*, or many things, like *hats*. We've already covered some of the rules for pluralizing *Count Nouns* in the previous section, **(p. 89)**

#5: Non-Count Nouns:

In contrast to Count Nouns, Non-Count Nouns *cannot be pluralized*. They include words like: *happiness, rage, spaghetti*. Non-Count Nouns are also often called *Mass Nouns*.

#6: Compound Nouns:

Compound Nouns are made of two or more nouns and may be used to convey a more specific meaning than any one noun could on its own. Some of these nouns are joined together as one word, as in *toothpaste*, while others are joined by a hyphen, as in *dry-cleaning*.

These examples and explanations should give you a basic overview of nouns and how they are used. Next, let's have a look at another very important and related part of speech, the pronoun.

#7: Pronouns

We've just seen what nouns are and what their basic roles are, so what's the meaning of something called a *pronoun*? Well, quite simply, a pronoun takes the place of a noun in a sentence.

Let's clear things up with an example.

David thought he saw a stray dog running through David's backyard, so David called out to David's wife, Shelley, asking Shelley to call animal control while David went outside in search of the beast.

Grammatically, this sentence is acceptable, but stylistically it's rather grotesque, isn't it? It refuses to let go of the Proper Noun *David,* and its redundancy creates a jarring effect on the mind of the reader. This sentence, therefore, could truly benefit from the use of a few pronouns.

David thought HE saw a stray dog running through HIS backyard, so HE called out to HIS wife, Shelley, asking HER to call animal control while HE went outside in search of the beast.

What a tremendously pleasing effect a few pronouns make! Simple, isn't it? Well, not quite, because in spite of the fact that pronouns seem simple to use, they are actually a fairly complicated part of speech. In fact, some grammar books devote large chunks of their pages to the analysis of pronouns and the roles they play in the language. This isn't the place for such an in depth analysis, however, (phew!), but we will take up a bit of space in order to explore the most common ones.

#1: The Personal Pronoun:

Personal pronouns are used in almost every sentence one speaks or writes. They refer to people or things.

Examples:
"Debbie lied! *She* said *we* could stay up with *her* until midnight!"

"Don't touch the cat's toy; *it* loves that thing."

Note: Although some may disagree on a moral basis, it is acceptable to refer to an animal as he, she, or it. Referring to a person as *it*, however, makes you sound like a psychopath, so unless that fulfills your goals, it's probably best to avoid calling Debbie an *it*.

Personal Pronouns include: I, me, you, he, him, she, her, it, we, us, they, them.

#2: The Possessive Pronoun:

Possessive pronouns are used to show ownership.

Examples:
"This is *my* car. That one is *yours*."
"That child is *mine*."

Possessive Pronouns include: mine, yours, hers, his, theirs, ours.

#3: The Demonstrative Pronoun:

Demonstrative pronouns are used to point, (demonstrate), things out.

Examples:
"Hey, look at *these*!"
"Is it *this* one or *that* one?"

Demonstrative Pronouns include: this, that, these, those.

#4: The Relative Pronoun:

In grammar, it's said that relative pronouns introduce adjectival or adverbial clauses. In practice, this is how they work.

Examples:
"I forgot *whose* shoes they are."
"He's the man *who* told me about the fish in the river."

Relative Pronouns include: who, which, that, whom, what, and whose.

A note: For clarity on when to use who and when to use whom, there is a quick discussion dedicated to it for easy reference later on. (**p. 167**)

#5: The Interrogative Pronoun:

Interrogative pronouns do exactly what they're named after; they interrogate!

Examples:
"*Who* said that?"
"*What*'s that supposed to mean?"

Interrogative Pronouns include: who, whom, which, what, whose.

#6: The Reflexive Pronoun:

Reflexive pronouns are pronouns that refer back to a noun or previous pronoun. It may sound complicated, but they're easy to spot since they typically end with either -elf or -elves.

Examples:
"Henry loves *himself*."
"Sandy didnt think she could do it, but she just kept telling *herself* to never give up."

Reflexive Pronouns include: myself, himself, herself, yourself, itself, yourselves, ourselves, themselves.

#7 The Indefinite Pronoun:

Indefinite pronouns refer to things that are unspecified. Remember our exploration of articles in the adjective section, (**p. 124**). In essence, indefinite pronouns serve the same function as the indefinite article.

Examples:

> "She said she wants *all* of them."
> "Gary gave Gail *everything* and she still wasn't satisfied."

Indefinite Pronouns include: all, another, any, anybody, anyone, anything, both, each, either, everybody, everyone, everything, few, many, most, much, neither, no one, nobody, none, nothing, one, other, others, several, some, somebody, someone, something.

#8: Verbs

Verbs, also often called predicates, are what make all of these parts move together to form an infinite amount of meanings. As such, verbs are complicated parts of speech, because their attributes and forms can be classified in many ways, and their base forms are conjugated in order to match the time the verb occurs.

Once more, though, let's remember the purpose of this text and simply provide an overview sufficient enough to get you writing without making common errors.

The first thing to know about verbs is that there are essentially only two types: *action* verbs and *linking* verbs.

The second thing to know about verbs is that you *must* have a basic understanding of what a *subject* and an *object* in a sentence is in order to understand how verbs function. Don't worry, it's a piece of cake!

Subject: The subject of a sentence is usually a noun or pronoun and can be determined by asking: *who or what is doing the action?* In the sentence: "David threw the ball." who is doing the action, (who is throwing the ball?): David. Thus *David* is the subject of this sentence.

Object: The object of a sentence is also usually a noun or pronoun and can be determined by asking: *to what or to whom is the action being done?* In the sentence: "David threw the ball." to what or whom is the action (to throw) being done: ball. Thus *ball* is the object of this sentence.

David, *the subject*, threw, *the action verb,* the ball, *the object*.

Good! With that out of the way, let's continue with our overview of verbs by starting with an examination of *action verbs*.

Action verbs can be grouped into one of two forms: a *transitive* verb, or an *intransitive* verb.

A **transitive verb** is one that *takes* an object. But what does that mean, exactly? Well, it means that the meaning or the action of the verb is incomplete unless it answers: *to what or to whom is the action being done?* To continue consistently from our previous example, stating that, "David threw," doesn't convey any meaning to the reader. To what or whom is the action (to throw) being done? In order to make sense, the writer must specify what or whom David threw.

An **intransitive verb** is one that *does not take* an object. An example of an intransitive verb is: "David fainted to the floor." Here, the verb, (fainted), cannot answer *to what or whom is the action being done*. It certainly isn't *the floor*, therefore, *fainted* has no object and may safely be deemed an intransitive verb.

"David fell from the tree." is another example that can be used to further highlight the characteristics of an intransitive verb. *To what or to whom is "fell" being done?* There is no satisfactory answer, thus *fell* is deemed an intransitive verb.

Tip: another way to determine whether a verb is transitive or intransitive is to temporarily replace the verb with: *did to what or whom*.

All right, so that's our quick overview of **Action Verbs**. Now, let's have a look at **Linking** verbs.

A **linking verb** is one that doesn't express an action, but a state of being. The vast majority of these verbs are a form of the verb *be*, as in *to be*, (*am, is, are, was, were, be, being, been, has been, should have been, may be, might be*), but there are others, including: *appear, seem, become, feel, sound, taste, grow, look, remain*.

Examples:
"I *am* a woman!"
"You *look* good today."

"The meat *tasted* spicy to me."

So, how, exactly, does a person go about determining if a verb, like *tasted*, is indeed a linking verb or not?
Simple!
If you can substitute a form of the *be* verb, such as: *am, was, is, are, were, being, been* — and the sentence still makes sense, then you've found yourself a genuine linking verb.

Example:
Original: "The meat *tasted* spicy to me."
Test: "The meat *was* spicy to me."
Test: "The meat *is* spicy to me."
Result: Confirmed Linking Verb!

Linking verbs can also serve another very important purpose in English, and that is to become an **auxiliary** or **helping** verb, which we will explore in the following section on *the tension of tenses* (**p. 147**).

So, you now have the basic overview of the 8 parts of speech of the English language. Understanding how these simple parts works together in order to form everything we've ever read and will read will go a long way toward ensuring that your own writings will accomplish the intended goals you set out for yourself in proper and correct grammatical form. Naturally, you're unlikely to remember the parts of speech simply by reading through them once or twice, so please, when in doubt, come back and re-read the explanations for your own good. If you need additional clarity on any of these subject, (and truly, some do go quite deep), consult a technical grammar book, or search for your answer on the internet.

Good luck and good writing!

<u>**Section 5:**</u>

Expansions On The Parts Of Speech:

Grammar is fine and all, but just learning what the parts are, although very useful, doesn't tell you much about *how* to use a lot of them properly in every day writing. Let's explore some tenets a little further.

The Principal Parts Of Verbs

In English, there are four *parts of verbs*, which is essentially the four forms a verb can take. These parts are:

#1: The Present Infinitive:

This is a verb in its "to" form, as in "to jump", "to play", "to scream" and is generally the form in which a verb is entered into a dictionary. It indicates an action taking place right now.

#2: The Past Tense:

This is a verb taking place in the past, as in "jumped", "played", "screamed". Notice how the verbs have changed from their present infinitive forms. These verbs are generally formed, (excluding irregular verbs, **p. 151**), by adding a -d or -ed to the end.

#3: The Past Participle:

This is a verb that also takes place in the past, and is also formed by adding either a -d or an -ed to the end, exactly like a verb in the past tense. The past participle, however, is ***not*** a tense, but simply a ***form*** of the verb. It is commonly used as an adjective: "He is a *divorced* man", "She has a *broken* heart", "Look at his *bored* expression."

#4: The Present Participle

The present participle is formed by adding -ing to the end of the verb, and it is used to indicate a continuing action. Just like the past participle, the present participle can be used as an adjective: "The sound of *driving* cars bothered him", "The *rising* sun brought us a welcome relief", "His *turning* swing will cause some damage in a storm."

<u>The Tension Of Tenses</u>

When writing, (or speaking), it's very important to be able to identify what *tense* the verbs you're using are in. More succinctly, it is crucial that the verbs you use are of the same tense. You use tenses every day of your life, with every sentence you speak or write, perhaps without even realizing it. There are three broad tenses in English: ***present, past, and future***. Within these, more specific categories exist in order to narrow down the *time frame* the verb occurs in, and these include: *simple tense, progressive tense, perfect tense,* and *perfect progressive tense*. Most people learn about tenses in elementary school when they learn to conjugate verbs.

Let's have a look at these common forms, using the verb "run" for demonstration.

	Simple	Progressive	Perfect	Perfect Progressive
	Habitual action	Ongoing action	Completed action	Combination of Perfect and Progressive
Present	Run	am/is/are running	have/has run	have been or has been running
Past	Ran	was/were running	had run	had been running

	Simple	Progres sive	Perfect	Perfect Progress ive
Future	will/shall run	will be running	will have run	will have been running

Here's a quick run through of each using the *present tense*:

- *The Simple Tense* expresses an habitual action, like: "I play hockey," or, "I eat a hearty dinner."

- *The Progressive Tense* expresses an ongoing action, like: "I am playing hockey," or, "I am eating a hearty dinner." The present progressive tense is always formed by using the **auxiliary verbs** *am, is, or are* and adding *-ing* to the end of the verb.

- *The Perfect Tense* expresses an action that's already been completed, like: "I have played hockey", or, "I have eaten a hearty dinner." Notice here how the verbs "play" and "eat" have changed in spelling. That's because the present perfect tense is always formed by using the **auxiliary verbs** *has or have.*

More on this in a moment.

- *The Perfect Progressive Tense* is a combination of the perfect and the progressive tense, and as such, expresses an action that has been repeated over a period of time in the past, that is ongoing now, and that will, presumably, be completed in the future, like: "I have been playing hockey", or, "I have been eating hearty dinners." The present perfect progressive tense is always formed by using the **auxiliary verbs** *have been or has been.*

This section should give you a clear overview of how verb tenses work. This section also relates back to the section on active voice vs. passive voice (**p. 61**), and helps to more clearly explains the difference.

A note on auxiliary verbs:

An auxiliary verb is defined as a "helping" verb, and it joins the main verb in order to express the tense and/or voice of the verb. You can see them in our examples above. Other common auxiliary verbs include: be, do, can, may.

The Irregularity Of Verbs

In our previous exploration of the adjective's and adverb's comparative and superlative forms, (**p. 84** & **p. 125**), we came across the special case of irregularities. So it is also true of verbs. As many English verbs can form their past tense and past participles by adding either a -d or -ed, (these are called regular verbs), to the stem verb, (the verb as found in a dictionary), there are many that cannot perform such a feat, and those verbs are called *Irregular Verbs*.

In order to conjugate these verbs into different tenses, just as with the irregular comparative and superlative adjectives and adverbs, their spelling must change in order to suit the tense.

Examples:

Stem (infinitive)	Simple Past	Past Participle
Break	Broke	Broken
Steal	Stole	Stolen
Freeze	Froze	Frozen

There are many of these verbs, and being aware of them when you see them will help ensure the sentences you write are always grammatically correct and in the tense you intend.

<u>Subject And Verb Agreement</u>

The subject of a sentence, (remember, *who or what is doing the action*), and verb *must* agree in number and tense. Thus, if you use a singular subject, you MUST use a singular verb. If you use a plural subject, you MUST use a plural verb.

<u>A Note:</u> This relates directly back to our previous discussion about using a plural pronoun to refer back to a singular personal pronoun, (**p. 105**)

<u>#1: Properly Identify The Subject:</u>

Difficulty and confusion often arises when someone incorrectly identifies the subject of the verb. For example, in the sentence, "A car full of people raced down the road," applying *who or what is doing the action* tells us that it is **car** and not **people** that is the subject of the sentence.

"A tray full of whisky shooters was spilled." The subject here, following the same test we've just performed, tells us that **tray** is the subject, and neither **whisky** nor **shooters**.

It is very important that the correct word is identified as the subject of the sentence, or else all sorts of unintended consequences will arise.

#2: When The Subject Identified Is a Pronoun:

By now you should know what the role of a pronoun is, but if you're still unclear, clarification can be found here, (**p. 133**). Now that you're clear, if the subject of a sentence is a plural pronoun such as: *you (as is "you people"), we, they, both, few, many, others, several,* you then MUST use a plural verb.

It may seem like an unnecessary repetition here, but this error occurs constantly in people's writings because it is sometimes subtle and somewhat common in popular culture, like in rap songs. If you aren't writing a hip hop song, do not incorrectly use a plural pronoun with a singular verb.

Examples:
> "We is the people you're waiting for."
> "They is the ones who started it."
> "Both is named Kevin."
> "Many people is upset about this."
> "Several men come down here looking for her."

All of these sentences are incorrect and will take away your writing's credibility if you make these mistakes.

<u>Take Care With Your Contractions</u>

This problem arises when a writer uses a contraction without thinking about it as a contraction.

Examples:
> "There's the books I bought today."
> "Here's the shirts I was telling you about."

If you take a moment to break these sentences down, you'll quickly find that *there's* and *here's* are contractions for *there is* and *here is*, thus making an incorrect agreement between the verb and the subject of the sentence. *There is the books I bought today,* and, *Here is the shirts I was telling you about* are incorrect because the linking verbs need to be plural.

Examples:
> "There *are* the books I bought today."
> "Here *are* the shirts I was telling you about."

With these few tips, you'll be well on your way to writing clear and proper English sentences.

<u>The Trouble With Then</u>

The word "then" is one of the most misused words in the English language. Like most common errors, it tends to arise from the way we speak in casual conversation. If you pay attention when reading, you'll come across sentences like this:

> "I called him, then I left."

> "She told me she'd done it, then she said that she wasn't sorry about it."

> "He says one thing, then says another that contradicts what he just said."

The problem with these sentences, (in bold for emphasis), is that the word *then* is **NOT a conjunction,** but an adverb. In order to properly write the above sentences you must first place a coordinating conjunction before the adverb *then*.

Examples:
> "She told me she'd done it, *and then* she said that she wasn't sorry about it."

> "He says one thing, *and then* says another that contradicts what he just said."

This is a subtle error that very often goes unnoticed, but it *is* a grammatical error that should be avoided in formal writing. Stay aware of how you're using the *adverb* then.

<u>The Conditional Sentence</u>

To expand on our previous discussion about how not to use the word then, (**p. 156**), let's now have a discussion about how to properly use it.

In English, one of the most common sentence structures you'll use, and see, is the *conditional sentence*, often referred to as the "if - clause." Its purpose is to discuss known factors and/or hypothetical situations and follow them with their applicable consequences.

If you pay attention, you'll notice that this book is full of conditional sentences. That last sentence, in addition to being true, is itself an example of a conditional sentence.

These sentence structures are of a complex nature, but their fundamental functions can be understood, as always, with a few explanations and examples.

The first thing to know about conditional sentences is that there are four types of them:
- The zero conditional sentence
- The first conditional sentence
- The second conditional sentence
- The third conditional sentence

Examples:
"*If* I see him, *then* I'll let him know."

"*When* she talks, *it's* time to listen."

The second thing to know about conditional sentences is that you need to pay attention to the verb tense, (**p. 147**), when using the different types of conditional structures.

The third thing to know is that you should generally always use a comma to separate the two clauses of a conditional sentence. Example: If this the first clause, then this is the second one.

The fourth thing to know is that, generally, the word "if" and "when" can be used interchangeably in order to begin conditional sentences.

#1: The Zero Conditional Sentence:

The zero conditional sentence is rather simple and straightforward to use as it generally expresses a truth or situation in which one thing *always* causes another thing to happen. **Be sure to use the simple present tense** when writing zero conditional sentences.

Examples:
"If you don't write, you don't get any better at it."

"If you brush your teeth, then your mouth stays healthy."

A common error, (and temptation), is to use the simple present tense for the conditional clause, (the first one), and then follow it up using the simple future tense. This is incorrect.

Example:

"If you don't brush your teeth, you *will* get cavities."

#2: The First Conditional Sentence:

First conditional sentences express situations in which the consequence, (second clause), is *likely* to be the result of the condition, (first clause), but isn't guaranteed. Take note of how the simple present tense is used in the first clause, but the simple future tense expresses the second clause, or consequence.

Examples:

"If you study, you will learn everything you need to know."

"If you practice, you will become a master of human communication."

Take care to not use the simple future tense in both the first and second clauses. The following sentence is incorrect:

> "If you will practice, you will become a master of human communication."

#3: The Second Conditional Sentence:

Second conditional sentences express consequences that are, typically, unlikely to happen. Here, the simple past tense is used in the first clause, and what's called an *auxiliary modal verb* in the second, which really only means that it uses words like: *should, could, would, might.*

Examples:
> "If I won ten million dollars, I would buy an island."

> "If I owned a bear, I would wrestle it."

<u>#4: The Third Conditional Sentence:</u>

The third conditional sentence expresses how the present circumstance(s) *would be* different if an alternate condition had been met in the past. They name conditions that could have just as equally occurred as the one that has, but didn't. To construct these sentences, you use the past perfect, (had + past participle), in the first clause, and a modal auxiliary, (would, should, could, might + have + past participle), in the second clause.

Examples:
> "If I *had applied* with better writing, I *would have gotten* that job."

> "If I *had made* better choices when I was young, I *could have been* rich today."

Thus, these are the basics of conditional sentences, a structure you're likely to use every day. Following the simple advice presented here should help you avoid common pitfalls and ensure that you are expressing yourself correctly and confidently.

We here conclude this section, expanding in various ways on the parts of speech in order to offer you additional tips on making the best impact you can when expressing yourself to others. The proper phrasing or structure makes all the difference when trying to stand out. "To be, or not to be, that is the question," is far more powerful and outstanding than, "The question is whether I should be or not." By understanding the parts of speech and the suggestions on style offered in this book will give you an enormous boost in the right direction. The rest is up to you. It takes practice, and it takes mistakes. Continue to learn and eventually, one day, like magic, while proof reading something you've written, you'll find yourself frowning, saying, "I can't believe *I* wrote this."

<u>Section 6:</u>

Common errors made when writing

Welcome! With the basic grammar out of the way, here is a somewhat short but no less important list of common errors people make when writing and/or speaking. Before you write, always take a moment to consider if the word you're using is in fact the word you're intending to use.

For your consideration:

- Alright vs. All Right:

Alright. It's everywhere, even in advertising, and it's incorrect. Yes, that's right! *Alright,* spelled this way, isn't even a word. Blew your mind, right? *Alright* is indeed two words, spelled: *All Right.* Now that all is right, let's move on.

- Explicit vs. Implicit:

These two adjectives are exact opposites, but some people commonly mistake one for the other.

Explicit, means to clearly express something with nothing left implied. It's the brutal truth, the meat and the potatoes, the harsh reality of things.

Implicit, on the other hand, means the exact opposite. It leaves things implied, not directly stated, open to discovery or interpretation by another party.

- Hung vs. Hanged:

This is probably one of the most common errors in the English language, and it makes sense why it happens so frequently. The verb "hang" in its present tense form, is an *irregular verb* (**p. 151**) and thus does in fact change to the past tense "hung" when referring to inanimate objects.

Examples:
"I hung the lights up last night."

"She hung her head in shame."

"They hung on every word of the speech."

All of these examples are one hundred percent correct.

When you're referring to _death by hanging_, however, the past tense and past participle (**p. 145**) of "hang" becomes "hanged". Thus:

"They hanged him last Monday morning."

"She hanged herself last year."

Only when "hang" refers to _death by hanging_ do you use the verb "hanged", otherwise, "hung" is the correct usage of the irregular verb "hang".

- They're vs. Their vs. There:

They're is the contraction of _they are._

Their is a possessive pronoun used as an attributive adjective, ex: their car, their school.

There is a versatile word used to indicate a place, "He's over there." Used to introduce a sentence, "There is no way." Used to express a state or condition, "I'll show you how to get started, but you're on your own from there." And it is used as an interjection, "There!"

- Who vs. Whose vs. Who's:

Who is an interrogative and a relative pronoun (**p. 133**), used mainly to refer to humans, "Who did this?", "Who is that woman?"

Who's is simply a contraction of *who is*, "Who's David speaking to?"

Whose is a possessive pronoun (**p. 133**), which also includes the variations, *whoever, whosoever, whomsoever, whosever.* "Whose car keys are those?", "Whose dog is running in our yard?"

- Who vs. Whom:

Whom is considered the formal form of the pronoun who, so how do you know when to use it over who? One general rule of thumb, and the one that is most often overlooked, is its use as a *prepositional complement*, meaning that if "who" is related to a preposition (**p. 121**), its form must be the *objective*, "whom".

Examples (prepositions in italics):
   "You were told that *by* whom?"

   "*To* whom did you send it?"

   "Whom are you referring *to*?"

As is demonstrated in the last example, it's important to consider if "who" is a *complement* of a preposition, and not just preceded by it.

- Let's vs. Lets:

   Let's is a simple contraction of "Let us".

   "Let's go!"

   Lets is the third person singular present tense form of the verb "Let".

   "He *lets* his dog out every morning."

- Arrogant vs. Ignorant:

This is a common error.

Ignorant means a lack of knowledge or training in a particular subject.

Example:
"He was ignorant of that law, but that doesn't excuse him from it."

Arrogant is used to refer to someone putting on an air of superiority or self-importance, someone pretentious, insolent, and overly proud.

Example:
"He was acting like an arrogant jerk."

- Affect vs. Effect:

Another common error people make is to confuse affect with effect, or vice versa.

Affect as a verb, means to produce a change in someone or something. It can also mean to pretend or fake an emotion or a behavior.

Examples:

> "The death of her mother *affected* her greatly."

> "He was quite *affected* after his car accident."

> "He asked me to *affect* a British accent."

> "She was merely *affecting* knowledge of the situation."

Effect is used to describe something that happened *as a result* of a cause or action.

Examples:

> "The only *effect* the sun had was to burn her skin."

> "She complained, but it had no *effect.*"

> "He thinks he'll be able to convince them to put his plan into *effect.*"

> "She wears all that jewelry for the *effect* it produces on her fans."

- Reel vs. Real:

This is an example of what's called an *Homonym*, meaning that they are two words phonetically pronounced the same way, but having different spellings and meanings.

Reel refers to an object like a spool or cylinder used to hold lengths of rope, hose, wire, film, etc. As a verb, *reel* means to put said rope, hose, wire, film onto a spool or cylindrical object.

Examples:
    "Hand me that *reel* of wire, please."

    "Reel in the line, my boy!"

Real refers to something actual, existing, in reality, whether physical or not.

Examples:
    "It may have been a dream, but it was still *real*."

    "I just can't convince myself that this is *real*."

- Talking vs. Speaking:

Both of these words essentially mean the same thing, but some people like to differentiate them by stating that *speak* is slightly more formal than *talk*. Furthermore, some definitions classify *talk* as a one sided discourse, while *speak* refers to a conversation between two or more people. There are no hard rules either way, and as is common in grammar, it's a matter of opinion and preference.

- Then vs. Than:

This is another common error and example of a homonym. Using the wrong "then/than" in your sentence can spell disaster for you, as the difference between the two is often considered basic and necessary for concise communication, especially in a formal or professional setting. Let's see the difference.

Then is most commonly used in relation to time, meaning furthermore, in addition, beyond.

"He kissed me and *then* we said goodnight."

Than is used when comparing things.

"Mine is better *than* his."

"I like metal music better *than* pop."

- Lose vs. Loose:

This error most probably arises solely due to the spelling. If you mean something that was lost, then you mean *lose*. If you mean something that was loosened, then you mean *loose.* Be certain of the quantity of o's you intend.

- Chose vs. Choose:

Again, a simple spelling error is most likely the cause of this confusion, but it is also made slightly more complicated by the fact that they are, indeed, variations of the same word, with the same definition.

Choose is the **simple present tense** form of the verb.
"I choose Sally to be on my team."

Chose is the **simple past tense** form of the verb *choose.*
"I chose Sally to be on my team."

A Note: For clarity on tenses, see, (**p. 147**).

- Accept vs. Except:

Accept means to take or receive something with approval.
"I *accept* your apology."

Except means to exclude something or someone from a group, or something else.
"Everyone was invited *except* for me."

- Allusion vs. Illusion vs. Delusion:

These words all sound similar, and two of them even mean similar things, but they are indeed three different, distinct words that each serve a specific purpose and have their own definitions.

Allusion means to make a passing, casual, and/or indirect reference to something else. Allusions rely on the recipient being aware or having knowledge of what it is that is being alluded to, otherwise, the meaning is lost.

Examples:
"The old man is as cheap as Scrooge."

"He's a real Sherlock that one."

Illusion refers to something that appears to be real, but isn't. Magicians, for example, specialize in the art of illusion. They make things seem to happen, like making an item disappear and reappear, when in reality they are only concealing and revealing the item. Illusion, in essence, means a deceiving or misleading impression of reality.

Examples:
> "Control over one's life is merely an *illusion*."

> "The investment opportunity was no more than a thin *illusion*."

Delusion is close in definition to an illusion, but it refers specifically to a false belief or opinion. A delusion is a false belief that offers, (at times enormous), resistance to appeals of reason or confrontation with actual, definitive, indisputable fact.

Examples:
> "He suffers from *delusions* of grandeur."

> "No matter the argument, the *delusion* persists."

- Less vs. Fewer:

Fewer is used only with **count nouns (p. 130)**.

Examples:
"There are *fewer* people there now."

"I have *fewer* ingredients involved in my recipe."

Less is used with **mass nouns (p. 130)**.

Examples:
"I have less money now than ever."

"We have less chance of success from now on."

- Borrow vs. Lend:

Although both of these words have to do with money, they represent two opposite actions.

Borrow means to **take** money as a loan.
"I *borrowed* five hundred dollars from my dad."

Lend means to **give** money as a loan.
"I am *lending* my son five hundred dollars."

- Cache vs. Cash:

Another homonym, but other than the pronunciation, they share nothing else in common.

Cache as a noun, refers to a hiding place. In computer science, a cache refers to a temporary storage space that allows for the limited storage and fast retrieval of commonly used files.

Examples:
"I'll just put this in my cache for a rainy day."

"It took longer because it was stored on disk and not in the cache."

Cash refers to physical currency.

Examples:
"I'll work for *cash*."

"You want these shoes? Fifty bucks, *cash*."

- Desert vs. Dessert:

This homonym is the cause of many errors.

Desert as a noun, refers to a vast, arid area of mostly sand and little to no water. As a verb, it refers to the abandonment of something or someone.

Examples:
>"He wandered aimless through the blistering heat of the *desert*."

>"They *deserted* her on the street."

Dessert refers to a usually sweet dish served as the final course of a meal.

Examples:
>"We have ice cream for *dessert*."

>"For *dessert,* we're having apple pie."

- Principal vs. Principle:

Principal refers to the head or director of a school, or, more generally, to the first or highest in rank, value, and/or importance.

Examples:
>"If you don't stop misbehaving, you will be sent to the *principal's* office."

"It is of *principal* importance."

Principle refers to a fundamental doctrine or tenet, a law or rule, a primary truth, or a personal basis of conduct or management.

Examples:
> "It isn't about the money, it's about the *principle*."

> "It is against my *principles* to accept this sort of behavior."

- Center vs. Centre:

Center with the "r" at the end of the word, refers to the middle of something. It can also refer to an establishment, or the core of something.
Examples:
> "He hit it dead *center*."

> "She fell right into the *center* of it."

> "We're off to the shopping *center*."

Centre with the "r" before the "e", is simply the British way of spelling the same word.

- Stationary vs. Stationery:

Sometimes, one letter can make all the difference in a word's definition.

Stationary refers to something that is standing still, unmoving.

Examples:
"The plane remained *stationary* for an hour."

"I was *stationed* outside the barracks all night."

Stationery refers to paper and/or writing materials including pens, pencils, paper, envelopes, etc.

- Irregardless vs. Regardless:

The only valid word of these two is the word regardless, which means to shows no regard for something or someone. The word *irregardless* likely comes from a confusion with the word ***irrespective*** which shares its definition with that of regardless, as in, without regard to something else, but especially to something specific, and it is often followed by the preposition **(p. 121)** *on.*

- Complement vs. Compliment:

These two words are close in both spelling and meaning, but they are indeed different.

Complement can be seen as a "companion" to something else, a helper, per se.

Examples:
"This wine perfectly *complements* the cheese."

"That jacket *complements* that skirt very well."

Compliment on the other hand, means to offer praise and/or appreciation.

Examples:
"An honest *compliment* is often all it takes to boost a lady's mood."

"He paid me the *compliment* of inviting me to go with him."

- Elicit vs. Illicit:

Elicit is a verb that means to draw out or bring forth something.

Examples:

>"He *elicited* a response by speaking harshly to her."

>"A reaction was indeed *elicited* in response to her brash requests."

Illicit is an adjective that refers to something that is illegal or unauthorized.

Examples:

>"Those are the *illicit* drugs they found."
>"Firearms are *illicit* in this country."

- Hone in vs. Home in:

>Is it "to hone in" on something, or "to home in" on it?

Hone is a verb that means to practice a skill with the goal of improvement.

Examples:

>"He is *honing* his writing skills."

>"She has *honed* her ability to tell the difference by now."

Home, as in, "to home in," means to find your, or its, destination. The expression you're looking for is indeed "To home in."

Examples:
> "The missile *homed* in on the target."

> "I *homed* in on the problem over time."

- Precede vs. Proceed:

The difference here is between a sentence that makes sense, and an awful lot of confusion.

Precede means to come before something.

Examples:
> "I will *precede* him in the ceremony."

> "I *precedes* e except after c, mostly."

Proceed means to continue with something, especially after having already stopped doing it.

Examples:
> "The reception will *proceed* after those men are escorted from the premises."

"Please, *proceed* with your presentation."

- Sell vs. Sale:

Two words so very similar, yet so very far apart.

Sell is a verb that signifies your intention to rid yourself of something in exchange for, (usually), money.

Examples:
"I'm *selling* my truck."

"I *sell* batteries for a living."

Sale is a noun which usually specifies a special disposal of goods at reduced prices, for a limited time only.

Examples:
"There's a big *sale* on at the mall."

"Everything in the store on *sale* for fifteen percent off."

- Site vs. Sight vs. Cite:

English can sometimes be confusing.

Site refers to an area or location.

Examples:
"I'll meet you at the *site*."

"This is the *site* of the accident."

Sight refers to the sense of sight, literally seeing.

Examples:
"You were nowhere in *sight*."

"I was *sighted* down in the valley."

Cite refers to the act of quoting a passage, book, author, etc., usually as an authority related to the subject at hand. As a noun, *cite* is referred to as a *Citation*.

Examples:
"Can you *cite* your source for this information?"

"I cannot accept a paper like this without *citations*."

- To vs. Too vs. Two:

To is a preposition which expresses a direction toward something, a person, a place.

Examples:

"*To* whom are you sending that email?"

"I went *to* your house but you weren't there."

Too is an adverb used to replace the word **also**.

Examples:

"You, *too*, have a good day."

"I want one, *too*."

Two is the number 2.

Examples:

"I'll take *two*, please."

"It was *two* and a half inches tall."

- Hoard vs. Horde:

Hoard as a verb refers to the stockpiling or accumulating of something that is kept secret or in hiding. As a noun, it refers to *what* has been stockpiled or accumulated.

Examples:

"He had a *hoard* of lumber in the back lot."

"She *hoarded* everything she got her hands on."

Horde is typically used as a noun to mean a large group or gathering of people or animals.

Examples:
"The *horde* of wilderbeast headed South from here."

"The *horde* of zombies decimated this part of the city."

- Farther vs. Further:

Some people like to use these words interchangeably. Those people are writing incorrectly. Luckily, their usage is fairly straightforward.

Use *Farther* for **physical** distances.

Examples:
"She's *farther* up the mountain."

"He's *farther* ahead in the race than I am."

Use *Further* for **metaphorical** purposes.

Examples:
>"I thought *further* about what you said."

>"Your arguments are *further* developed than hers are."

- Diffuse vs. Defuse:

Defuse means to literally take the fuse out of a bomb. It's also used metaphorically.

Example:
>"She *defused* the situation."

Diffuse means to spread out or scatter widely, as a fluid, or smoke.

Examples:
>"The ink *diffused* in the water."

>"The smoke *diffused* thinly throughout the room."

- Pour vs. Pore:

Pour is a verb that refers to the act of pouring, or spilling something like a liquid from a bottle or other container.

Examples:

> "He *poured* the gasoline onto the fire."

> "*Pour* me a glass of whisky, please."

Pore as a verb refers to reading or studying something with absorbed attention. As a noun, it refers to the tiny dilating openings in skin, (among other things), that is used for perspiration.

Examples:

> "That cream blocks my *pores*."

> "Sweat oozes from the *pores* to cool you down."

- Flair vs. Flare:

Flair refers to a natural talent or ability, or a keen perception.

Examples:

> "She's got a *flair* for writing."

> "Sports are not his *flair*."

Flare refers to a bright blaze of fire used as a signal.

Examples:
>"They found him after he fired a *flare* into the air."

>"In case of accident, mark road ahead with *flares* for your own safety."

- Breach vs. Breech:

Breach refers to a breaking or opening in of something.

Examples:
>"The water *breached* the dam upriver."

>"The soldiers *breached* the wall with a savage determination."

Breech refers to the hinder or lower part of anything, most commonly used to refer to a birth.

Example:
>"They performed a caesarian because the baby was in breech position."

- Tortuous vs. Torturous:

Tortuous refers to something that is full of twists, turns, and/or bends. A path, road, or way that is not straightforward or direct.

Examples:
> "It was a *tortuous* path through the woods."

> "Just follow the *tortuous* road up the mountain."

Torturous refers to something that pertains to, involves, or causes suffering.

Examples:
> "The play was *torturous* to watch."

> "They *tortured* the truth from him."

- Assure vs. Ensure vs. Insure:

Assure means to express certainty, usually positively, in order to comfort or secure against doubt or uncertainty.

Examples:
> "He *assured* her that she'd pull through the surgery without any complications."

"She *assured* him that she could do it."

Ensure means to secure or guarantee something, to make something certain.

Examples:
"This ticket will *ensure* your seat on the plane."

"I will personally *ensure* the safety of your vehicle."

Insure means to guarantee something against a potential loss or damage.

Examples:
"I have *insured* the boat for forty thousand dollars."

"Do you have proof of *insurance*?"

- Breath vs. Breathe:

These two words are often confused. It's important to differentiate between the noun and the verb.

Breath is a noun which refers to the air being inhaled and exhaled during respiration.

Examples:

"Just take a *breath* and calm down."

"It knocked the *breath* out of me."

Breathe is the verb which refers to the act of respiration itself.

Examples:

"Can you *breathe* at this altitude?"

"The secret to squatting is your *breathing*."

- Capital vs. Capitol:

Capital is regularly used to refer to various things, some of which include the town or city that is the official location of the government, wealth, and the act of capitalization of letters.

Examples:

"Canberra is the *capital* of Australia."

"This business needs an injection of *capital* in order to expand."

"The first letter of any sentence is always *capitalized*."

Capitol refers to a specific building in Washington D.C., which is used by the Congress of the United States Of America.

- Empathy vs. Sympathy:

The definition of these two words are often confused. When writing, be sure you're choosing the one you mean.

Empathy refers to a person's ability to place themselves in someone else's situation, or to face an imaginary problem in order to determine how they would react if it were real.

Examples:
> "You need to have *empathy* in order to write convincing characters."

> "The man lacks all *empathy*, that's why he's capable of such horrible actions."

Sympathy refers, generally, to feelings of compassion toward another person in trouble, pain, need, etc. It can also refer to the mere agreement of feelings between one person and another.

Examples:
> "My deepest *sympathies* for your loss."

> "I *sympathize* with your situation, but there's nothing I can do."

- Lay vs. Lie:

One of the most common errors in English is the misuse of "lay" and "lie". The solution to this common conundrum is to understand the difference between transitive and intransitive verbs (**p. 139**) and between the present and past tenses (**p. 147**).

Lay, which refers to put or place something or someone, is an transitive verb, (it takes an *object*).

Lie, which refers to rest or recline, is a transitive verb, (it takes no *object*).

- Seen vs. Saw:

This is an error in the same vein as the difference between lay and lie.

Seen is the past participle, (**p. 145**), of *see.*

Example:
"I have *seen* that house before."

Saw is the simple past participle, (**p. 145**), of see.

Example:
"I saw that house yesterday."

- Alot vs. A lot:

This one is fairly simple to remember.
Alot **is not a valid word**. It doesn't exist, therefore, do not use it. Ever. Anywhere.

A lot is the proper spelling you're looking for.

There are many more words that are often confused in English, and this isn't by any means an exhaustive list. If you're unsure, a quick internet search is sure to point you in the correct direction.

The point here is that you, as a masterful communicator and writer, should *never* assume that a word is correct without being one hundred percent sure. Taking a moment to check will go a long way to ensuring you avoid embarrassment and potential loss as a result of rushing and assuming your correctness.

Like every other skill in life, aim to be precise and certain.

<u>Conclusion</u>

In your hands you hold one of the major keys to the success of your blog, your ad, your difficult letter to your employees, or the simple work-order you need to fill out. Any opportunity to write is an opportunity to practice what you've learned in this book.

Beware, however, and do not fall into the fallacy of believing that just because you've skimmed through this text once or twice you are now a master of communication and any failure that befalls you from now on isn't your fault, but the fault of this book, which clearly wasn't very useful to you.

As previously stated, learning to write is a process. It's a skill, and skills take time. They take practice. No one learns to play the piano in a week, or even a month, but by accumulating bits of related patterns and knowledge every day, eventually, fingers begin to dance along the keys with minimal effort.

This book was designed to accomplish three things. The first is to teach, and the second is to serve as a reference guide so that, as you're writing your next blog post or important email, you can take a moment at the first glimmer of doubt and check the appropriate section to see if your intuition is indeed correct. The third is to help you realize the importance and potential power contained in the language you use every day. By being aware of this potential, and by using the guiding principles in this book, you can accomplish anything you want simply by being better able to describe your ideas, goals, feelings, and plans to yourself and to others. Words truly are magical when they're used with intent and directed at a particular target.

Well structured sentences and proper words are the key to being taken seriously in the world, to being heard, to being considered authoritative, honest, confident, capable, and intelligent. Here are the keys to attracting more readers to your blog, more customers to your website or company, increasing sales through your marketing, being considered for the positions you apply for, getting your employer's attention with your suggestions, and a host of other situations where simply knowing how to write will give you a clear advantage over your potential competitors.

Once basic grammar and sentence structures are fundamentally understood, you will begin to see the potential for injecting your writing with even more creativity, and how structures can be manipulated to form even more complex feats of language. And with that, in addition to the skills you'll learn, you will also find that you suddenly have an entirely new level of enjoyment available to you while reading novels, or any other type of book. When reading a master novelist, you will be able to truly appreciate the hard work and absolute brilliance some people have been able to achieve simply through the manipulation of words and sentence structures.

Writing is a nebulous thing, difficult to teach beyond guiding suggestions and grammar. In fact, like all other skills, it is something that needs to be learned largely on your own, through trial and error for a continued but focussed amount of time regardless of your skill level, because you can always push yourself further.

The truth is, the only way to truly learn to write at an expert level is to read voraciously. Books are your masters, your guides, your keys to glimpsing possibilities you hadn't considered and hadn't thought possible. If you can learn to appreciate books as more than just entertainment and focus on appreciating the skill involved in writing some of them, you will find yourself in a new world, glancing about with fresh eyes at a profundity you hadn't realized was all around you before, and being able to express what you now see will launch you into the stratosphere of whatever endeavor you choose to pursue.

So welcome to a new world. Use the skills taught in this book to your advantage and get to where you want to go. Visualize it in your mind, find the correct words to describe it, then find some better words, combine them in various ways until you find that one combination that really pops by conveying *exactly* what you feel, what you mean, and then use it to focus on your goals.

You can do this.

Get started right now.

Great Human Skills
www.greathumanskills.com

Tombstone Kane
www.tombstonekane.com

www.ingramcontent.com/pod-product-compliance
Lightning Source LLC
Chambersburg PA
CBHW060749050426
42449CB00008B/1325